Blackb

Teaching Assistants

Practical

Strategies

for Effective

Classroom

Support

Maggie Balshaw and Peter Farrell

David Fulton Publishers

London

David Fulton Publishers Ltd
The Chiswick Centre, 414 Chiswick High Road, London W4 5TF

www.fultonpublishers.co.uk

First published in Great Britain by David Fulton Publishers 2002
Reprinted 2002, 2003
10 9 8 7 6 5 4 3

British Library Cataloguing in Publication Data
A catalogue record for this book is available from the British Library.

ISBN 1-85346-828-2

Typeset by FiSH Books, London WC1
Printed and bound by The Thanet Press, Margate.

Contents

About the Authors

Dr Maggie Balshaw is an independent educational researcher and consultant. Amongst her publications is *Help in the Classroom* (David Fulton Publishers 1999) a book that has become a standard text for staff development courses on teaching assistants. She also coordinates projects focusing on inclusive practice development nationally and internationally, using the Unesco teacher education resource pack *Special Needs in the Classroom* (Unesco 1991).

Professor Peter Farrell is Head of the Educational Support and Inclusion Research and Teaching Group in the Faculty of Education, University of Manchester. He has had a long-standing interest in research and development in the whole area of inclusive education and has published widely in this area.

Both authors directed a project funded by the DfEE into the Management, Role and Training of Learning Support Assistants, the findings of which were published in 1999. Work that stemmed from the report of the project forms the basis for this book.

Acknowledgements

There are many people we would like to thank for making it possible for us to publish this book. In particular, Ianthe Wright and her colleagues from the Teaching Assistants and School Support Team in the DfES invited Maggie to advise on the development of the Good Practice Guide on Working with Teaching Assistants. In addition they offered financial support for a series of seminars for teachers aimed at publishing the Guide as widely as possible. Their continued support for the development of the role of TAs in schools and LEAs has been most welcome and has helped raise the status of this relatively new group of professionals.

We would also like to mention the schools and LEAs who took part in the pilot project that led to them developing the work of TAs in their own contexts. Without their hard work, initiative and enthusiasm it would not have been possible to write this book. We are particularly grateful to them for allowing us to use evidence of their work as case examples of good practice in Section 3, the appendices and website of this book.

Cheshire LEA

Upton Priory Junior School: Ann Parr, Karen Woodall, Kath Sayers, Kath Everitt
Puss Bank Infants School: Catherine Mattocks, Maggi Simmons (now Puss Bank Primary)
Park Lane School: Helen Chadwick, Pat Redding
Ryles Park High School: Rosemary Bamford, Sam Hulme, Carolyn Ashcroft
Officers: Fintan Bradley, David Richards

Harrow LEA

Grange First School: Lynne Sumner, Brenda Gibson, Sharon Smith
Vaughan First and Middle School: Sue Nilsson, Surinder Minhas, Jackie Millington
Visual Impairment Sensory and Communication Team: Elizabeth Clery, Janice Allen, Rosie Downing, Jaquie Lawrence, Kathryn Lees, Margaret Banger
Whitmore High School: Karen White, Anne Perring, Sneha Radia, Angie Lawrence
Officers: Jackie Harrop, Elaine Gardner

Salford LEA

Parkes Field School: Lynn Monks, Angela Macdonald, Jane Walsh, Tinah Clarey (now Springwood School)
Moorside High School: Dave Winning, Marie Sinclair, Yvonne Gibson
Primary Partnership Service: Yvette Wright, Sarah Lindley, Linda Sales
Officer: Judith Jones

N.B. This is a list of participants who took part in research meetings (i.e. 'lead' researchers) and does not include the many others (TAs and teachers, senior staff and governors, parents and pupils) who worked within the schools and services on the research. We duly acknowledge the important contribution that all of them made, particularly the assistants.

Introduction

In recent years teaching assistants (TAs) have begun to play an increasingly important role in helping schools and LEAs to improve the quality of education for all children. Traditionally their work has almost exclusively been associated with helping in the education of children in special schools. Subsequently they have developed a crucial role in supporting mainstream placements for pupils with statements of special needs. More recently, however, their increasing contribution towards assisting in the education of all pupils has been recognised. These developments have posed many challenges for the TAs themselves and for those involved in employing, managing, supporting and training assistants. In particular senior staff in schools and LEAs are now required to plan induction training for TAs, to support their continuing professional development, to prepare and review job descriptions and to deploy them in schools so that they can work effectively with and alongside their teacher colleagues.

The main purpose of this book, therefore, is to describe and review ways in which senior staff in schools can develop management strategies for working effectively with teaching assistants. These strategies are directly linked to the Good Practice Guide (GPG) that was first published in October 2000. This guide (DfEE 2000a) builds on the findings of a DfEE-funded research project into the management, role and training of learning support assistants (Farrell *et al.* 1999).

Approaches that are suggested in the book are supported with real examples from practice, showing the reality of how schools can review and develop practice and so become more effective in their management and support of teaching assistants.

Specially the aim of the book is to enable:

- managers in schools and LEAs to work effectively with teaching assistants

- teachers to plan classroom approaches to working with teaching assistants

- teaching assistants to improve their practice

- children to learn more effectively in inclusive settings

Throughout the book we show how the findings from the Manchester research, that were the stimulus for the development of the GPG, have been used to help schools engage in action research projects that have led to improvements in the work of TAs in schools and LEAs. This is in line with the aims of the GPG itself, which are to provide a development tool for staff to use to improve the work of TAs in schools. The book will therefore help senior staff in schools and LEA support staff to develop their own strategies for effective work in this area.

The book is divided into four sections. In Section 1 we provide the background and context of the whole book. The two chapters in this section trace the origins of the rapid growth in the number of TAs and place this within the Government's twin agenda of raising standards in education and developing inclusive practices. We also review the key findings from the Manchester research and describe how they were used to develop a set of key indicators and review questions that related to effective practice in working with TAs. We show how the findings from this project informed development work on the GPG. We end this section with a description of how we managed a series of pilot action research projects in three LEAs, the findings of which form the basis of the accounts in Section 3.

The three chapters in Section 2 examine the conceptual bases that underpin the key strategies referred to in the GPG, through discussing the findings from the Manchester research in more depth. These strategies inform approaches that can be used in schools and support services to bring about improvements in the work of TAs. This provides a framework for senior staff to manage and support TAs effectively.

Section 3 begins with an explanation of the strategies schools can use within the action research approach that underpins the GPG and the Manchester research, to bring about whole school improvements in relation to the work of TAs. This is followed by a series of chapters each of which draws from the findings of the pilot projects to illustrate ways in which schools and support services can work with TAs to improve their work in this important area.

The final section, Section 4, considers some of the key themes that have emerged from both the Manchester research and the pilot projects in relation to the ways in which schools can bring about whole school developments in effective practice with TAs. It is illustrated with reflective accounts of assistants involved in the pilot research and what this has meant to their working lives. In addition there are nine Appendices illustrating the descriptions in the chapters and on the website, www.fultonpublishers.co.uk which is used to provide more extensive examples of the work done in the schools and services.

We hope this book will act as a stimulus for senior staff in schools and support services to continue their efforts to develop effective ways of working with teaching assistants in schools and classrooms. It should be used as a source of ideas to stimulate development work in primary, secondary, special schools and LEA support services.

Section 1
Background to the development of the Good Practice Guide

1 Recent Developments in the work of teaching assistants

Overview

In the past few years the developing role of assistants and the growth in their numbers has attracted a great deal of publicity. The Government has stressed the vital role they can play in supporting the whole process of education. Indeed, there are even suggestions that assistants might in the future take over some of the teachers' tasks. However, some anxiety has been expressed by teaching unions about the effects this might have on teachers' professionalism. Therefore, instead of being seen as a valuable resource to support teaching and learning in schools, TAs could now be viewed as a threat to the development of the teaching profession.

Our view, which is reflected in all of the chapters throughout this book, is that the whole process of teaching and learning requires effective teamwork between teachers and assistants and that each group can support the other. Teachers have a pivotal role in the planning and management of the educational process. Their work can be enhanced greatly through working collaboratively with TAs and as a result all pupils can benefit. Our research indicates that the majority of TAs do not want to take on additional responsibilities that are rightly associated with the teacher's role.

The rise in the number of TAs now working in schools should therefore be seen as a positive development. Indeed a number of research projects, in addition to the Manchester research, have reported on the benefits that TAs can bring to schools (see for example Smith *et al.* 1999; Lee and Mawson 1998; Mencap 1999). Furthermore there are several books and journal articles that report on the developing work of TAs (see for example Rose 2000; CSIE 2000; Thomas *et al.* 1998). There are also a number of books that are devoted exclusively to ways in which teachers and assistants can work together to support pupils. Of these perhaps those written by Balshaw (1991, 1999), Lorenz (1998) and Fox (1993, 1998) have had the most impact.

Recently the Government has also recognised the valuable and supportive role that TAs can play. The Good Practice Guide (DfEE 2000a) is only one example of this. Others include the two sets of induction training materials for newly appointed TAs in primary and secondary schools (DfEE 2000b; DfES 2001). These are available in every LEA and are being used extensively. In addition the Government have supported the work of the Local Government National Training Organisation (LGNTO), which has recently devised a set of occupational standards for TAs (LGNTO 2001).

Figures tracking the actual rise in the numbers of TAs suggest that initially the growth was due to the increase in the numbers of pupils with statements being educated in mainstream settings. The 1997 Green Paper *Excellence for All Children: Meeting Special Educational Needs* (DfEE 1997) suggested that there were 24,000 full-time equivalent teaching assistants working in mainstream schools and that this number was expected to rise. Indeed the rise in the numbers of TAs working in mainstream schools mirrors schools' and LEAs' growing commitment towards inclusion.

Building on these developments a subsequent Green Paper, *Teachers: Meeting the Challenge of Change* (DfEE 1998), refers to the projected increase of 20,000 in the number of classroom assistants who will provide general support in mainstream schools that is not restricted solely to pupils with special educational needs. In addition the Green Paper refers to the need to recruit and train 2,000 'literacy assistants' to help in the implementation of the Government's literacy strategy. The CSIE (2000) estimate that there are now as many as 80,000 TAs working in mainstream schools. Recently the Government has announced that further funding will be made available until 2002 and beyond to employ more than 20,000 TAs making the total number to be in excess of 100,000 and this figure excludes those who work in special schools. Indeed it is now not uncommon for there to be as many assistants as there are qualified teachers in many primary schools. We have also visited secondary schools where there are over 20 TAs undertaking a range of varied and often quite complex tasks.

Conditions of service for TAs

An issue of growing concern among all professionals working in education is that conditions of service for TAs are inadequate, particularly in comparison with teachers, and do not in any way reflect the highly skilled work that they are required to undertake. This is dealt with in more depth in the next chapter when we review the findings and implications from the Manchester research. Problems associated with temporary contracts, low levels of pay and limited opportunities for career progression are well known. However at the present time the Government has indicated that issues of pay and conditions of service should be managed at a local level. It is therefore unlikely that there will be a nationally agreed pay scale linked to career progression and training, at least in the near future. Consequently, managers and other senior staff in schools and LEAs will continue to be required to use their skills of mentoring and support so that their workforce of TAs can work effectively and with enthusiasm. Indeed one of the aims of this book is to help such staff to develop their work in this area even though the current conditions of service in which TAs work are far from adequate. As this book will show, there is a great deal that senior staff can achieve through supporting and working with their TAs to bring about improvements in the education of all children.

The training of TAs

In addition to problems with conditions of service for TAs, concerns have also been expressed about training opportunities. It is not, for example, uncommon for a TA to be appointed to support a child with autism in a mainstream school who has never met an autistic child before, who has had no prior training and who may have no further education beyond GCSE/O levels. Once again the implication of the training issue will be covered in more detail in the next chapter. However, it is important to point out at this stage that there have been several initiatives at local and national level that have attempted to address this problem. Chief among these is the new induction training programme developed by the DfES, referred to above. In addition there are a whole range of accredited courses run mainly by colleges of further education but also by universities and LEAs. Finally the Local Government National Training Organisation (LGNTO) has supported the development of national occupational standards for TAs which became available in autumn 2001. These indicate the competencies (in NVQ terms) that TAs should possess at two levels, those of a recent entrant into the profession and those of a more experienced assistant.

It is possible that in the future there will be a nationally agreed set of qualifications for TAs that will be based around the NVQ framework and that this will be complemented by a full range of short courses covering a range of areas from induction to more specialised training in a specific area. These developments should help managers and senior staff in schools and LEAs to work with their TAs in planning a coordinated and ongoing programme of training aimed at meeting the needs of the TAs themselves, teachers and other relevant staff.

Developing more inclusive practice and the work of TAs

In mainstream schools the increasing number and expanding role of assistants reflects, in part, a growing national and international movement to make educational provision more inclusive. Assistants therefore have the potential to play a key role in helping to make inclusive education effective for all pupils including those with statements. For this reason it is important to reflect on current developments in inclusive practices so as to understand how TAs can work most effectively within an increasingly inclusive system.

The term inclusion evolved out of earlier concepts of integration or mainstreaming; terms that were used solely to refer to the placement of pupils with special educational needs (SEN) in mainstream schools. One problem with defining integration solely in terms of provision (i.e. the setting in which a pupil is placed) is that it tells us nothing about the quality of the education that is received in this provision. Are pupils placed in units attached to a mainstream school, for example, more 'integrated' than if they were taught in a special school? Jupp (1992) argued that such units can be just as segregating. Similarly a pupil with SEN placed in a mainstream class may in fact be isolated from the rest of the class and not truly 'integrated' within the group, particularly if he or she works with an assistant in one-to-one sessions for the majority of each day. Integrated placements, therefore, may still leave the pupil 'segregated'.

For these reasons the term 'inclusion' has become a more accepted way of describing the extent to which a pupil with SEN is truly 'integrated'. Essentially, in relation to pupils defined as having SEN, the term refers to the extent to which a school or community welcomes all pupils with disabilities as fully inclusive members of the group and values them for the contribution which they make. For inclusion to be effective all pupils must actively belong to, be welcomed by and participate in a mainstream school and community – that is they should be fully *included*. Their diversity of interests, abilities and attainment should be welcomed and be seen to enrich the life of the school.

Recently definitions of inclusion have broadened still further (see for example Booth and Ainscow 1998). These writers take the view that policies on inclusion should not be restricted to the education of pupils thought to have special needs. Inclusion, they argue, is a process in which schools, communities, local authorities and governments strive to reduce barriers to the participation and learning for all citizens. Looked at in this way inclusive policies and practices should consider ways in which marginalised groups in society, for example people from ethnic minorities and those who are socially and economically disadvantaged, can participate fully in the educational process within mainstream contexts.

This view has been strongly endorsed by the recently published *HMI Guidance to Inspectors* (Ofsted 2000). This advises HMI on what to look for when assessing the extent to which a school is developing effective policies and practices on inclusion. According to the guidance 'Educational Inclusion covers

- Equal opportunities (for all pupils regardless of age, gender, ethnicity, attainment, background);

- The education of pupils having English as a second language;

- The education of pupils with special educational needs – including pupils with challenging and disruptive behaviour;

- Pupils who are gifted or talented.'

This document, above all others, affirms a view of inclusion that has developed far beyond one which focuses on the education of pupils thought to have SEN. In future schools will be judged by the extent to which they are inclusive. Indeed the Guidance states that 'The most effective schools are inclusive schools.' Inclusion is therefore at the heart of the Government's education policy along with its commitment to raise standards.

As referred to above, the increase in the number of TAs working in schools has paralleled developments in thinking on inclusion and raising standards. Indeed, the Good Practice Guide refers to HMI reports that have 'confirmed the tremendous contribution that well trained and well managed teaching assistants can make in driving standards up in schools.' TAs therefore have a major contribution to make in helping the Government to achieve its objectives to raise standards for all pupils within an inclusive framework.

What's in a name?

Professionals working in education and parents over the past few years cannot fail to have noticed that the name given to assistants seems to vary from school to school, from LEA to LEA and from country to country. Indeed sometimes assistants in the same school can have different names. In one primary school in which we worked as part of our research for the DfES, there were no less than four 'types' of assistants each with a different name. Those who supported a small group of pupils with severe learning difficulties were referred to as 'resource school integration assistants', those who supported children with moderate learning difficulties were referred to as 'learning support assistants', there were also two 'classroom assistants' and a 'nursery nurse' who worked in the infant department.

Figure 1.1 indicates the different names we encountered, in our research and from reading the literature, that were used to describe staff without teaching qualifications working alongside teachers in the classroom.

Nursery Nurse	Teacher's Aid	Special Support Assistant
Learning Support Assistant	Para-professional Assistant	Classroom Assistant
Non Teaching Assistant	Bilingual Assistant	Teaching Assistant
Resource Integration Support Assistant		Special Needs Assistant

Figure 1.1 Different names given to assistants working in classrooms

One might legitimately ask whether the name given to assistants is important, provided their role and function are understood by all concerned. However, we believe that the name can send an important message to teachers, parents and LEA administrators and that there are good reasons for settling on one name only, a name that conveys the correct message about their work within an inclusive framework.

There are names included in Figure 1.1 that convey an inappropriate message. For example 'nursery nurse' seems anachronistic even for those who work in nursery schools or reception classes in infant schools. These staff, who may have the NNEB qualification, do very little nursing and the term has uncomfortable medical connotations. The same could be said of the phrase 'para-professional' used widely in the United States; again the prefix 'para' has medical overtones. 'Special support assistant' suggests that the assistants are only employed to work with students who have SEN and therefore seems inappropriate within an inclusive framework. The term 'teacher's aid', also popular in the USA, has caused some unexpected misunderstandings when, for example, an announcement over the school's intercom requests that all teachers *'with aids'* should come to a staff meeting! Finally the label 'Non-Teaching Assistant' implies that the assistants do no teaching! What is more, should a formal title on a job description begin with a negative such as 'non'? It is hardly likely to lead to positive self-esteem.

Giving different names to assistants can imply that one group with a particular name has a higher status than those who are given a different name. We have evidence that this has led to there being unfortunate jealousies and rivalries within a school when, for example, assistants who work with pupils with special needs feel that they are in some way superior to other assistants partly because they are referred to as 'Special Support Assistants' rather than 'Classroom Assistants'.

We take the view that the name should convey a message that assistants are employed to assist the teacher in all areas of education from pre-school to school leaving age. Their name should not restrict them to working with one group, e.g. pupils with special needs, or imply that they are not employed to teach but are just required to undertake less exacting tasks, e.g. tidying the paint cupboards. The Good Practice Guide stresses the Government's wish to use the term 'Teaching Assistant', and this seems appropriate given the range of tasks that TAs are now undertaking. They may, of course, develop specialisms in, for example, teaching pupils with visual or hearing impairments. However, they will still be TAs first and foremost. Those with additional skills and responsibilities will hopefully receive recognition for this through being placed on a higher grade. In this way their status will mirror that of teachers who, after all, are also 'teachers' first and foremost although many develop specialisms and gain promotion; but while they work in a school they are always a *teacher* of one kind or another.

It should be pointed out, however, that in the examples of work with TAs in schools and services discussed later in this book, a number of different terms are used to describe the work of assistants. These were the terms they used at the time and we therefore have adopted them in our discussion to provide greater authenticity to the accounts.

2 The origins of the Good Practice Guide

Key findings from the Manchester research

In July 1998 the DfEE commissioned the Faculty of Education at the University of Manchester to carry out a research project into the Management, Role and Training of Learning Support Assistants. The final report (Farrell *et al*. 1999) contained details of the main findings together with a set of indicators and review questions that were intended to be used by staff in schools and LEAs as a development tool to bring about improvements in the work of TAs in schools. The key findings informed the development of the indicators and review questions. Therefore in this part of Chapter 2 we summarise the main findings from the report and in the next we describe how we piloted the indicators and review questions that ultimately have provided the practical examples that make up Section 3 of this book. Many of these findings relate to the work of TAs with children who have special needs and this is mainly because the scope of the research focused on this group. However, as we have stated earlier, TAs work with all children and not just those with disabilities and it is our view that the findings of our study are applicable right across the education spectrum. (Note: as we have adopted the Government's preferred term 'Teaching Assistant', we use this or 'TA' when referring to the report's findings, although the original report refers to learning support assistants, LSAs.)

The qualifications and experience of TAs

The findings of our study confirm previous research (e.g. Smith *et al*. 1999) in respect of the gender, previous work experience and qualifications of TAs. Of the 147 TAs we interviewed, only seven were men. Many lived locally and had school-aged children. Being a TA was a more attractive alternative to working in a shop or a factory because of the school holidays, free weekends and relatively short working day. The vast majority of TAs had no paper qualifications related to working with young people although, as mothers, many had experience of looking after children. A small number of TAs had qualifications in related subjects (e.g. nursing) and a few had psychology degrees. Headteachers stated that when employing TAs they looked for good interpersonal skills and the ability and willingness to work as a team.

The role of TAs and class teachers

A general finding from our interviews suggested that there was a clearly understood distinction between the roles of TAs and teachers. Teachers are responsible for the overall success of the teaching programmes; they plan the work, monitor the pupils' progress, plan review meetings and liaise with parents. Meanwhile, TAs are seen as being responsible for implementing the programmes under the teachers' guidance. TAs were, on the whole, happy to work in this way. Although they all wanted to be involved in discussions about planning and implementing teaching programmes, they did not want to take full responsibility for the success or failure of their work. The vast majority believed that the teachers were responsible for the pupils' progress and would be the ones to be held to account if there were problems.

Our classroom observations and discussions with a few TAs indicated that this frequently stated distinction between the role of TAs and teachers in respect of the planning and implementation of programmes was not quite so clear cut in practice. In general, where there was no specialist teacher with a direct responsibility to support TAs working in mainstream schools, TAs tend to be given more opportunities to develop their skills in adapting programmes of work and in planning new programmes. For example in one secondary school much of the detailed work on literacy was taught in a withdrawal situation and appeared to be planned by the TA.

Time for planning

A major issue raised by teachers and TAs was the lack of time for joint planning. Although teachers felt responsible for directing the work of the TA, this could only be effective if sufficient time was made available for programmes to be planned and reviewed together. Too often both teachers and TAs complained that the lack of planning time meant that neither knew what work a child was supposed to be doing at the start of the lesson. However, in some cases we found that planning time had indeed been identified and used productively, with positive outcomes.

Styles of support

The style of support offered by TAs in mainstream classes was remarkably similar across all mainstream schools visited. In general they kept regular contact with pupils they supported but did not sit with them throughout a lesson unless he/she was working on a completely different curriculum area from that of his/her peer group. Both pupils and TAs preferred to work in this way. Many pupils clearly did not want their problems to be highlighted in front of the rest of the class through the TA spending too much time with them.

In contrast to the similar styles of support being provided within a mainstream class, a wide variety of practices were observed in relation to withdrawing pupils from class for individual sessions. For example some pupils with specific literacy difficulties in primary and secondary schools were withdrawn for extra work on literacy skills while others were supported in class as were most of the primary-aged pupils with severe learning difficulties whom we observed. In general teachers and TAs adopted a flexible approach to this issue and were responsive to pupils' wishes.

The way support is provided to pupils with SEN in mainstream schools is central to the debate about developing effective inclusive practices. As suggested in the previous chapter, if pupils with SEN are supported on a full-time basis by TAs who only work individually with them throughout the day, it is difficult to argue that this is an inclusive way of working. Indeed such practices may prevent them from making contact with their peer group and hence they become segregated within the school and the presence of the TA serves to accentuate this position. Alternatively many pupils with SEN have particular problems in learning that require them to receive one-to-one attention for parts of the day, otherwise they will not learn. It is therefore vitally important for programmes of work to combine individualised instruction, either in class or on a withdrawal basis, with supported group work in mainstream classes that encourages the pupils to be included within their peer group. This balance of work is not easy to achieve and inevitably some compromises have to be made. TAs and teachers therefore need to be sensitive to the needs and wishes of all students and to review the situation frequently.

A further issue related to the styles of support concerns the role of the class teachers in working directly with pupils with SEN. There were teachers interviewed in our study who took the view that the TA was employed solely to work with a child with SEN and that their role was to work with the other children. On other occasions, however, we observed teachers and TAs sharing some of the work both with children with SEN and with the remainder of the class. For example the teacher might work individually with a child with SEN or with a small group, leaving the TA to support the rest of the class. Our data suggested that teachers, TAs and pupils preferred this more flexible way of working and considered that it was an essential step towards developing more inclusive practices.

The views of class teachers about TAs

As teaching in the UK has traditionally been an activity that has gone on behind closed doors with teachers working alone without the presence of another adult, we were interested in obtaining their views about working with TAs. We were encouraged to find that all the teachers interviewed were extremely positive about having TAs in their class. 'We could not manage without them' and, 'It's essential for inclusion to work' are just two of the comments that were made. Well over three-quarters felt they had the confidence to work with assistants though they recognised that this required them to plan more carefully and to develop teamwork skills. Two teachers in a secondary school considered that a minority of their colleagues (particularly the more experienced ones) were less happy about working with TAs in the classroom. However, with increasing inclusion and the growing number of TAs being employed, they felt that all teachers would develop more positive attitudes towards TAs in the near future.

The views of TAs about their work

A striking feature of all the interviews with TAs was their enthusiasm for the work they do. Over 95 per cent stated that they enjoyed their work and felt that they were making a genuine contribution towards helping pupils with and without special needs. They also felt that staff, parents and pupils valued their work. In particular they valued the opportunity to get to know a relatively small number of pupils really well, much more than a class teacher normally does. This positive attitude towards their role does not take account of their concerns about salary, conditions of service and training, issues that are considered below.

When asked if they would like to be teachers approximately 80 per cent of the 147 who were interviewed said that they would prefer to remain as TAs. The main reason for this was that they did not want to take on the additional tasks and responsibilities associated with teaching. Around 60 per cent saw teaching as being a stressful profession and had no desire to work the additional hours that are expected of teachers. 'When I finish work, I want to go home and forget about school' was a remark which reflected a sentiment expressed by many. However, younger TAs, in particular the 10 per cent with degrees (e.g. in psychology) or with other qualifications (e.g. in nursing) expressed the desire to move on to other professions. They saw their work as a TA as a way of filling a gap between their degree and gaining a place on a social work or counselling course. Three TAs with psychology degrees were interested in becoming teachers and were applying for places on teacher training courses.

Conditions of service for TAs

A major concern expressed by all those interviewed was the whole issue of TAs' contracts and pay. Levels of pay, typically around a third of a teacher's salary, were seen as being far too low when set against the work that TAs undertake and the responsibilities they are given. All TAs resented this. As one ruefully remarked, 'You couldn't live on this salary.' 'I would get more working at a supermarket check out,' said another. They all felt that pay differentials between themselves and teachers (often as much as £14,000 per year) were far too large and that the differences in their roles were not so great as to justify this huge imbalance. Teachers and senior managers also believed that these pay differentials were totally unjustified given the work that TAs were expected to do.

Around half the TAs we interviewed were on temporary contracts that were linked to a pupil with SEN whom they supported. If the pupil left the school their contract could be terminated. Understandably this caused a great deal of anxiety among the TAs concerned. Contracts also specified how many hours TAs were supposed to work and, in most cases, these hours coincided with the time the pupils were in school. As a result, if TAs came in early or stayed late, they received no extra pay. Despite this major disincentive to work a few extra hours that could be used for meetings, training, planning or preparation, many TAs were prepared to do so even though they received no extra remuneration.

In addition to problems with contracts there is also little or no career structure for TAs in the schools and services we visited. All those we interviewed saw this as a major problem. There were, however, examples in mainstream secondary schools where the post of senior TA had been formed and in most cases these staff were paid slightly more than their colleagues were. These posts were created because the TAs in question had worked for several years in the school and were recognised for their outstanding contribution. Generally these senior TAs were well respected and they took on additional management responsibilities in relation to their junior colleagues. For example in one school the senior TA, in addition to managing the team of two TAs, was responsible for liaising with parents and outside agencies, the LEA and feeder schools. In another, where there was a senior and deputy senior TA, they took on the training and induction of TAs and managed the timetable, and they were given non-contact time for this work. In a third school an experienced TA helped to coordinate a reading programme which involved direct contact with parents, and she had timetabled time for this.

The training of TAs

A central theme running through responses to a questionnaire and from the interviews was the need to develop a coordinated and nationally recognised pattern of training for TAs that was linked to career progression. Only a tiny minority of TAs had received any accredited training that was related to their work prior to entering the profession. One TA felt very strongly about this and considered that a basic entry qualification was needed otherwise 'anyone can enter the profession'. She believed that currently the profession is devalued, as the job is perceived as being one that anybody could do.

An increasing number of schools and local authorities have recognised this problem and now offer a series of short in-service training courses. Others have begun to plan more extensive accredited courses. All TAs we interviewed welcomed the opportunity to attend training programmes not least because the invitation alone was a recognition of their status in the school. In addition several felt that training was essential in order to help them to meet the needs of the vulnerable pupils they were supporting.

Since the publication of the report there have been further developments in the training opportunities now available for assistants, in particular the DfES induction package for use in primary and secondary schools. Although it is still too early to judge the impact of this initiative, anecdotal evidence suggests that they have been welcomed by the TAs and the schools in which they work.

In addition to the DfES initiative the TTA has published a booklet providing the names and addresses of institutions offering training to assistants who wish to enhance their qualifications and become teachers (TTA 2001).

Summary: A definition of effective practice

The findings of this DfEE study are relevant for the future development of the work of TAs, particularly in view of the expected increase in the numbers entering the profession over the next few years both in the UK and elsewhere. In order to shape future developments one overall aim of the research was to draw on the findings to begin the task of defining effective practice in this complex area of work. At a very general level the results suggested that effective practice in the work of TAs involves contributions that:

- foster the **participation** of pupils in the social and academic processes of a school;
- seek to enable pupils to become more **independent** learners;
- help to **raise standards** for all pupils.

This is a view of the work of TAs that is fully integrated within the school system, where they are not committed solely to working with individuals who have special needs, and where their key role is to encourage all children to be fully included in the community of the school. This requires TAs to work as a member of the whole school staff team and to be valued for the contribution they can make.

Piloting indicators of effective practice in schools

The definition of effective practice, referred to above, was the starting point for the development of a set of key indicators that were presented in the final part of our report (Farrell *et al*. 1999). These are presented in Figure 2.1. Each of these indicators was accompanied by a number of questions that were designed to help staff to focus on issues that were directly related to each indicator. [The terminology in this set of indicators, drawn from the 1999 report, is LSA.]

The indicators and review questions were intended to be used as a staff development tool to bring about improvements in the work of assistants in schools and LEAs. However, they had not been 'tried and tested' when the report was published. Consequently we initiated a small-scale action research project in which we worked with staff in three LEAs to pilot the indicators and review questions in schools to see if they could act as a stimulus for change.

We invited Salford, Cheshire and Harrow LEAs to take part in the pilot research and held preliminary discussions with a lead officer from each authority. They then discussed the aims of the research with selected schools and support services and from this process mainstream schools (primary and secondary, some of which had additional provision) and special schools and support services from the LEAs volunteered to participate. A more detailed description of our work with these schools and support services is presented in Chapter 6.

At the same time that the schools and services were working on their action

---

A: *The Role of LSAs*
A1   LSAs work co-operatively with teachers to support the learning and participation of pupils
A2   LSAs work with teachers to prepare lesson plans and materials
A3   LSAs contribute to the evaluation of outcomes of lessons
A4   LSAs make relevant contributions to wider school activities

B: *The Management of LSAs*
B1   Teachers' management strategies provide clear guidance as to how LSAs should work in their classrooms
B2   Schools have policies outlining the roles and responsibilities of LSAs
B3   LEAs ensure that LSAs' conditions of employment foster effective practice

C: *Training*
C1   Teachers and LSAs learn together to improve the quality of their work
C2   School staff development programmes foster the competence of LSAs and teachers to carry out their respective tasks
C3   LEAs provide relevant training and support for LSAs
C4   Use is made of institution based courses or courses run by voluntary organisations to extend the expertise of LSAs

---

Figure 2.1 Indicators of effective practice in the role, management and training of LSAs

research projects, staff from the DfES Teaching Assistants and School Support Team were working on an early draft of the Good Practice Guide (GPG). Indeed, staff from this team attended one of the follow-up workshops that were linked to our action research project. In addition one of the authors of this book (Maggie Balshaw) worked on the team that was advising the DfES on the content of the GPG.

As readers will know the GPG suggests that the nature of support that can be provided by TAs can be divided into the following strands:

- support for pupils,
- support for teachers,
- support for the curriculum, and
- support for the school.

This vision of the work of TAs sees their role as being entirely integrated with the whole process of education and development for all children. They should be part of the whole staff team and not be seen as a marginalised group who only work with individual children. In order to translate this vision into reality the GPG refers to six main areas of good practice in the work of assistants that provide a starting point for managers in schools, support services and LEAs to address when trying to bring about improvements in the work of assistants. These six areas are:

- Defining responsibilities clearly,
- Providing clear deployment within a flexible framework,
- Creating partnerships with teachers,
- Supporting effective liaison with other people involved in education,
- Developing teamwork among teaching assistants, and
- Reviewing performance and promoting development.

These are each linked to a set of indicators and questions, many of which are the same as those in the Manchester Report although they are organised differently. The 'essence' of our questions remain a key part of the Good Practice Guide, despite its framework being characterised as being related to 'management issues'. Furthermore the Guide has adopted the definition of effective practice in working with TAs that was included in our report (see above).

Following the publication of the GPG in autumn 2000, Manchester University, together with the DfES, ran a series of six seminars in the early summer of 2001 that were aimed mainly at senior teachers in schools and LEAs. At each of these seminars, staff from schools and services that took part in the pilot research, including TAs themselves, talked about how they had used the indicators and review questions from the Manchester research to bring about improvements in the work of TAs. Indeed it was a strength of the seminars that many of these accounts were led by assistants from the schools and services. Some of them form the basis for the examples that are presented in Section 3 of this book. The overall aim of the seminars was to help participants consider ways in which the GPG could be used as an effective staff development tool to bring about change in their own setting.

This brief review of the development and origins of the GPG and how this was linked to our original study provides the background for the remainder of this book. In the next section (Section 2) we discuss in some depth the rationale behind many of the key features of the Guide, through referring in more detail to the findings from the original Manchester research. This provides a conceptual context for Section 3 in which we describe and comment on innovative development work that took place in the schools and services from three LEAs that took part in the pilot research.

Section 2
Developing a conceptual framework for improving practice

In Section 2 we reflect in more depth on aspects of the Manchester research that relate to the development of effective practice in the work of TAs and to the key sections of the Good Practice Guide. Chapter 3 considers aspects of our findings that are linked to 'defining responsibilities clearly and providing clear deployment within a flexible framework'. Chapter 4 discusses effective practice in relation to 'partnerships with teachers and working with other individuals in education'. Chapter 5 reviews ways of 'developing assistant teams, and reviewing performance and promoting development'. In this way we provide more detailed illustrations from the Manchester research that can inform the conceptual basis for the practical examples that follow in Section 3.

3 Defining responsibilities clearly and providing clear deployment within a flexible framework

This chapter considers the issues associated with the development of clear responsibilities for TAs, the ways in which they might be involved in this process and how the outcomes are communicated to the rest of the team, particularly class teachers. The chapter goes on to address the ways in which flexible deployment of the assistants may be achieved, in order both to play to their strengths and to enhance the learning environment for children. It draws on the Manchester research evidence in these key areas of management practices.

Devising clear responsibilities

Job descriptions

A key issue for managers and assistants to consider when employing TAs is the role and relevance of job descriptions. Our research indicated that there were several important basic requirements of the role that managers considered *before* employing TAs in the first place and were therefore a prerequisite for a job description. For example being competent in basic literacy and numeracy was a common requirement, particularly at primary level. At secondary level there was evidence that previous experiences of working with young people before in some related capacity was seen as particularly relevant.

Managers with responsibility for initially employing assistants in schools and services had clear criteria for the skills and competencies they wished to see in assistants. In some cases parents also had clear ideas as to what skills and abilities were needed to be an effective TA, as did some of the students we interviewed during the course of the research.

In terms of clearly devised roles and responsibilities for TAs within a flexible framework there were several key issues. Where assistants, particularly in primary schools, had originally been volunteers, parent helpers or dinner-time supervisors there was an ongoing need to be sure that the developing job did not become too demanding for them in terms of what they had originally agreed to do. Assistants who were very good parent helpers do not necessarily develop or wish to develop into skilled staff in, for example, supporting the literacy and numeracy strategy. Headteachers in the schools where the most effective practices in this area existed had recruited different assistants with clear baseline criteria. Where existing staff wished to apply for these posts they were asked to make a clear commitment to training or re-training to meet the needs of the schools on re-recruitment.

Deciding on appropriate entry criteria to the profession is an important first step in developing job descriptions. In our research, however, we found examples of effective practice where job descriptions were clear and explicit and others where the job had evolved but was still clearly understood and agreed upon by all concerned.

Where job descriptions were explicit and up to date assistants felt clear about their responsibilities and the tasks they undertook. They were confident that other colleagues, including the teachers they worked with, also had a working knowledge of the work they were required to do. The job descriptions therefore indicated the ways in which they were expected to support pupils (as individuals or in groups); the tasks they undertook in support of teachers and also their wider responsibilities in terms of the curriculum and the school as a whole. Interestingly in these settings assistants felt more confident about questioning inappropriate requests.

We also found a few schools that had recently revised and redefined job descriptions for TAs and had involved the assistants themselves in this process. These were then discussed with senior managers and in some cases with LEA personnel or governors in order to agree their suitability. Some schools had piloted them before settling on an agreed format. One consequence of involving TAs in revising job descriptions was that they felt much more confident about the definition of their roles.

However, it must be remembered that there are still schools where statements such as 'Well yes, I have got a job description somewhere, it's the LEA one, I got it about six years ago when I joined the school' are not uncommon. This can lead to assistants working in an atmosphere of uncertainty or ambiguity, or working in narrowly focused ways that don't help them professionally and are probably inappropriate for the children with whom they work. As one assistant said not long ago, 'I feel as if I'm making it up as I go along!'

There were of course many examples where the role of the TA had evolved over time, where the original job description was effectively redundant but where all staff, pupils and parents were clear about the work that they did and happy to see their role evolve to suit changed circumstances. A key example of this evolution of the role of TAs is in the impact of the literacy and numeracy strategy in primary schools. Here, particularly following the introduction of the strategies, TAs' roles had been widened to encompass support in these areas.

A further and more complex example stemmed from a move from one assistant being seen as 'attached' to one child (in many cases reflecting the contracts of employment they were issued – particularly in respect of support for a statement of special educational needs). Although it is common for TAs to be assigned to support a child with a statement in mainstream school, it is now commonly accepted that to be effective in supporting a pupil, it is important for the TA not to be glued to the child and to spend time with other children as well. Their role therefore becomes more flexible.

Further to this, in respect of the relationship between the contract, the job specification and the statement, there had been a growing realisation in some schools and LEAs that it was acceptable for a child's statement to refer to the number of hours of 'support' without inferring that, in the majority of cases, this meant that only one individual assistant carried out this role. This assistant could be potentially then seen as a 'fixture' in regard to the individual child.

When questioned about this sense of attachment the children themselves had varying opinions. However, most of them, even quite young ones, sought to be separate, independent and, crucially, working with their classmates and friends. For example, 'She doesn't always sit with me (or our group), but she's over the other side, helping someone else but she keeps "an eye out" – if I need help she comes.' And as one fifteen-year-old put it, 'We don't need them in practical subjects like science or agriculture. They sometimes walk round behind us. It's a nuisance!'

This comment is particularly relevant in respect of secondary schools, where students meet a variety of subject teachers. They feel that the constant presence of a 'supporter' across the curriculum does nothing for their independence and chances of fitting into a secondary school culture, and does untold damage to their 'street credibility' with other students. Another valid comment often made was of the following kind: 'She supports me in English and history, I'm good at maths and science, I don't need her,' a clear recognition that the student was aware of his own needs. Many schools have now recognised this strength of feeling, and with exceptions for certain individuals who have high levels of personal need and may need a 'key supporter', have moved to more flexible forms of deployment.

Another factor in the largely redundant job descriptions was schools' increasing skills in deploying assistants more flexibly as they became more confident in their work and, indeed, as school managers began to develop different and sometimes innovative strategies. This was particularly significant where the team working in support of individual pupils/students was seeking ways to encourage better participation in overall classroom and curriculum experiences. This recognition had also led to the need to make sure that pupils were getting more opportunities to work more independently, relying on reducing amounts of the TAs' direct support.

It is clear from the above discussion that job descriptions for TAs have evolved considerably over the years and that the specified tasks and duties that were laid down at the start may no longer be appropriate. TAs have an important part to play in writing and revising job descriptions, provided they evolve and develop with the full understanding of all involved, including the parents and the pupils. This review may be built into appraisal processes, an issue dealt with in Chapter 5.

Developing flexible strategies

One aspect of the successful evolution of job descriptions is the importance of developing flexible strategies in the management and support of assistants. Our research indicated that where more flexible forms of deployment had occurred, a number of management strategies had been used to facilitate this. Senior managers in schools provided clear line management and coordination of the assistants' work. The co-ordinators of the staff development programme had paid attention to the needs of assistants in planning school and staff development. Funding, usually from the standards fund, to a portion of which the assistants were entitled, had been earmarked, protected and in some cases used in very flexible ways. There will be more explanation of this in Chapter 5.

Managers had also taken some steps in some schools to ensure that teachers were familiar with the assistants' job specification in order that a consistency of deployment occurred and fewer teachers were asking assistants to carry out inappropriate tasks. In particular, teachers were not asking assistants to work with a pupil or group of pupils that they either did not wish to work with or felt incompetent to work with themselves. In order to support the work of teachers, some attention was paid to their training needs in respect of managing another adult in the classroom, whilst drawing these adults into classroom teamwork in such a way that the teacher and assistant formed an effective working partnership. The detail of planning for classroom teamwork and forms of classroom organisation that supported this had also begun to be addressed through these strategies. The next chapter deals in more detail with these issues.

An element of this was encouraging classroom and subject teachers to play to the particular strengths and skills of assistants in order to support the curriculum. Meeting the needs of pupils through this curriculum support became an important flexible strategy so that in many schools assistants were becoming confident, competent and skilled in supporting selected areas of the curriculum. In the primary schools this tended to focus on literacy or numeracy, and in some cases areas like music or art. In secondary schools it had led to faculty or subject department links and attachments. Where appropriate, and for some individuals, the assistants' particular knowledge of pupils' progress or an individual's achievement was also a focus for them to address and managers made it clear that this was expected of them.

As this brief overview indicates, having clear job descriptions that can be applied within a flexible framework is one of the cornerstones of effective work of TAs. In the remainder of this chapter we discuss further examples of how working in this way can help to overcome potential barriers to inclusive practice, promote independent learning and raise overall standards of pupil achievement.

Potential barriers to inclusive practice

In respect of encouraging more flexible ways of working in the classroom a number of features were noted in the schools where practice was well developed. In particular it was evident that both teachers and assistants had paid attention to the need for participation in the curriculum on offer for all children. This was in relation to three major issues.

Participation with peers

It is vitally important to ensure that the way in which the assistant works does not form a barrier to a pupil's participation in experiences and learning with peers. This can happen in quite subtle and non-planned ways. For example, an assistant with one child or a small group of children can work in such a way that she forms a barrier to those children being able to mix and work with and learn from the rest of their classmates. Where a teacher directs an assistant to work for virtually a whole lesson with the same child(ren), and sometimes for more than one lesson, those children experience a barrier to opportunities for learning with and from many or most of their peers. In secondary schools it is possible for some students never to work with the majority of their classmates, because they are always in the same group, which has been determined because of the presence of the assistant.

Direct teacher attention

Secondly, an associated barrier that schools have become aware of is that of the assistant being a barrier to some children receiving direct teacher attention. The teacher makes an assumption that there is a small group of children for whom the teacher does not have responsibility. They are 'the assistant's group'. In this way the teacher does not manage the learning of all the children directly, but only takes responsibility for the majority. Schools that are aware of this danger have realised that two things follow. One is that the more vulnerable children work with the 'least qualified' person for large parts of the day or week. The other is that the teacher's teaching strategies remain the same and the teacher does not develop skills needed to successfully teach all the children in the class.

Overall classroom processes

The third barrier that can also be experienced is where the children in 'the assistant's group' do not engage with the overall classroom processes. These might include whole class teaching points; changing the pace of the lesson; a class review of progress; setting parameters, targets and timescales; and a reflection on learning as a class. All these activities might go on without drawing in the group for whom the assistant has responsibility, leaving them to experience a different kind of lesson from their peers altogether.

These three areas of concern had been addressed by managers, teachers and assistants in many of the schools we visited during the research. They had done this using a problem-solving approach working in teams. They sought contextually useful solutions and tried them out with varying degrees of success. They refined them from lesson to lesson, depending on the successes experienced. None of them were 'off the shelf' solutions, but took account of the context, the particular needs of the children, the children's ideas of how it worked for them and so on.

The schools where managers and teachers had developed more flexible strategies, particularly in respect of the deployment of assistants, have learnt that the three pitfalls mentioned above should be avoided at all costs. Otherwise pupils will not receive their entitlement to learning from the teacher and their peers as well as the assistant. Each of these potential barriers to inclusion can set up 'in-class segregation'.

The discussion of the definitions of integration and inclusion, provided in Chapter 1, are illustrated in these examples. They show that the development of classroom practice and alterations to basic approaches to teaching are often the crux to developing more inclusive practices at the classroom level and ultimately within school as a whole.

Promoting independent learning: contractual issues

Over the past few years there have been contextual features that have mitigated against TAs working to enhance the development of pupils' independent learning. One is the nature of the contracts on which many assistants have been employed. Because of the allocation of statements to an individual child, contracts have been issued by LEAs on the basis of an allocation of one-to-one support. In addition most of these have been, and some continue to be, temporary contracts, up for review, with a possible reduction in hours of work and potential redundancy. Schools have therefore been wary of demonstrating that the assistant has done a very positive job, supported the child in such a way that s/he has become an independent learner, and the assistant is, therefore, no longer needed! The 'Catch-22' situation has been, in a nutshell, 'If you are really good at your job, we'll make you redundant!'

However, schools that have created flexibility around the role have become much more confident in promoting independent learning for children, and indeed, in some cases have striven to make sure that dependency should only happen briefly and be phased out as rapidly as possible. They have encouraged assistants to build in forms of child-to-child support, drawing in peer support rather than adult support for those individuals who have higher levels of need. The way support is planned by teachers, as classroom managers, has led to the flexible deployment of the assistants' time in such a way that they can demonstrate (to the LEA if need be) that the TA has been working in one-to-one support as required on the statement but that this has not been in ways that builds in dependency on that support.

There was evidence in at least two of the research schools that the school's determination to alter the status quo on this had led their LEA to alter its practice in respect of the wording on statements and how contracts were issued. Many schools and LEAs have now moved away from temporary one-to-one contracts for assistants, thus creating a climate where producing independent learners does not lead to wholesale redundancy, but to enhanced learning opportunities.

Raising standards of achievement

Some of these enhanced learning opportunities have come about from a further development in strategies for flexible deployment. For many primary schools this was triggered by the introduction of the national literacy strategy. Teachers, when interviewed, said that they had begun to think more creatively about how to use their assistants' skills, competencies and knowledge. This creativity and wider deployment led to considering flexible deployment at other times of the school day than just the literacy (and later numeracy) hour. In addition through breaking away from narrowly focused individual education plans delivered by the TA, teachers began to work more flexibly with their assistants. Several teachers explained how they had really rethought much of their planning and organisation because of this. Thus standards of achievement for children had been raised as teachers had become more skilled at planning joint approaches across the curriculum.

In secondary schools this move had been much more marked at an organisational level. Schools that had developed effective practice deployed their assistants to faculties/curriculum areas. There were three reasons for doing this. Firstly, they had identified subject areas that assistants felt interested, confident and comfortable to work within. They had sought to play to these strengths by allocating assistants to related faculties/curriculum areas.

Secondly, they had in this way eased an organisational problem of the number of staff with whom assistants have to make links, relationships and plans. Meetings in one faculty that are held reasonably regularly are organisationally simpler than attempting to build links across seven to ten faculties. The assistants also have opportunities to get to know teachers better and to form professional relationships with them outside the classroom as well as in it. This has been a positive experience and reduced 'strangeness' sometimes experienced by TAs on entering classrooms.

Thirdly, it has reduced the students' perceptions and misperceptions about support being a threat to their 'street credibility'. They meet assistants/supporters as members of faculty teams rather than as individual helpers who appear in many of their lessons, but do not have a real grasp of the curriculum on offer.

Detractors from these strategies will say that they reduce continuity for individuals and have the effect of watering down their support. Moreover, they may also say that it is good for the assistant to 'experience the lesson from the student's perspective', then they can make the necessary adjustments to instructions, tasks, materials, etc. What this in effect leads to, however, is that the assistants 'paper over the cracks' and the teachers never or seldom make the necessary adjustments to their teaching strategies in order to make the lesson or subject accessible to all the learners in the classroom. Thus the status quo is maintained, the students may be 'integrated' to some degree, but this is at the expense of the development of truly inclusive classroom cultures.

Playing to assistants' strengths

In concluding this chapter it is important to emphasise one further feature of the development of TAs' roles and responsibilities within a framework of flexible deployment. This is the recognition of the need to play to the existing strengths, interests and skills of the assistants.

Many assistants have worked in other forms of employment than education. Many teachers have not, although this has changed considerably over recent years with school leavers taking gap years or periods of other work before seeking qualified teacher status. The incidence of mature recruitment has also risen. There is now a great deal of evidence to show that, used wisely, creatively and flexibly, the skills assistants bring into the school from other jobs and experiences such as parenthood can enhance the capacity for curriculum support in many ways that complement and extend the existing skills of teachers.

In the schools that have learnt to use these skills creatively assistants who have been laboratory technicians, managers of shops, charity fundraisers, policewomen, librarians, silver service waitresses and swimming instructors, to name but a few examples, have enhanced, in all kinds of ways, the curriculum experiences of many children. For example, the shop managers have brought numeracy and accounting skills into the maths curriculum; charity fundraisers have used their PR skills in supporting students in developing approaches to running school businesses, and their design skills from writing/drawing eye-catching posters and advertisements; policewomen have contributed to the development of managing confrontation in devising the behaviour management policies of the school... and so on.

An over-reliance on more traditional ways of deploying assistants' skills can lead to narrow uses of their time, an emphasis on their skills being used to counter deficits, either perceived in children, or missed in teaching strategies, and an over-reliance on their caring and compensatory skills. These latter do have a relevance for some children, often in concentrated periods of time, but seen as a major focus of the assistants' work can reduce opportunities for learning and the quality of that learning experience.

In conclusion, in this chapter we have provided an overview of some issues related to clear roles and responsibilities and flexible deployment, with many examples drawn from the practice observed and discussed during the Manchester research. The next chapter goes on to explore the issues of how teachers and assistants might develop effective partnerships and how assistants make good working connections with others who are closely involved in the education of children in their school or service.

4 Creating partnerships with teachers and working with other individuals in education

This chapter considers the following issues: how to establish effective working partnerships between teachers and assistants, how both partners can learn from each other, and how effective links can be established with governors, parents and other professionals working in and with the schools and services. The discussion draws on the findings from the Manchester research and indicates that the schools we observed had spent a considerable amount of time working out ways of improving their work in this area. The sections that follow illustrate that the solutions lie in working creatively and flexibly in specific contexts with staff (including managers) who are committed to effective assistant/teacher teamwork and who understand that this is an important component of good practice in working with TAs.

Developing teamwork

There was evidence in the schools and services that we studied that there were some key factors leading to more effective teamwork, particularly in respect of teachers and assistants sharing classrooms. They had developed joint understandings of their aims and purposes when working together. They had clear ideas about the amount, type and depth of the assistant's involvement at various stages of the lesson. They had discussed what was needed to make sure all pupils were getting access to the curriculum and also how to manage continuity between lessons.

Teachers and TAs had also discussed the needs of individuals and groups and how to make sure that pupils experienced a variety of approaches to teaching and learning with both of them working with the pupils over whom there was particular concern, for example those with individual education plans. They talked about how to meet the needs of particular pupils with disabilities and their strategies for supporting access. They had thought about forms of peer support and ways of arranging groups so this could happen as well as adult support. They were clear about their joint approaches to managing behaviour and how to respond to any challenges presented to them.

Planning in partnership

What this all meant, of course, was that they had planned these strategies. They had done this on a long-term, medium-term and immediate level. As one Key Stage 3 teacher said, 'Since I've discussed with the assistant what we should do I've become much clearer in my own mind about outcomes that I want for all the children. I really miss it at times of the day when she's not around, I've got so used to the feedback and good ideas!' Another primary teacher said that, since the literacy strategy had been introduced and he and the assistant had planned how they would implement it, he now had much more flexible ideas about how to make the best use of the assistant's skills and ideas at other times and in other curriculum areas.

Many of the assistants interviewed in primary schools were very sceptical, and indeed critical, about the additional literacy strategy (ALS), which gave no provision whatsoever for planning time with teachers. Some of them who were doing some of the ALS part-time and working on a more school-led basis the rest of the time said that the difference in the planning time for the school's own programme of support, even in the literacy strategy itself, was considerable. They felt the other approach to be extremely short-sighted, and in the end counterproductive, and this really brought home to them, and the teachers with whom they worked, the importance of planning time.

A key component of planning is reflecting on feedback from the children and from each other about what they have managed to do together. Developing confidence in taking feedback is not always easy for teachers and some of those interviewed admitted that it was 'scary at first', but that once they had got used to it, it was fine. They elicited information from their assistants about classroom organisation and the strategies they had both used, as well as feedback about certain pupils, as a matter of course. It became a valued facet of their classroom planning.

This confidence had for many of the teachers also made them comfortable in altering plans and developing flexibility during the lesson, consulting with the assistant about changes they might make in response to the ways in which the pupils were reacting to what they were doing. This flexibility in teamwork tended to develop as teachers and assistants had become more comfortable in their work together. Part of this is because of the teacher appreciating what the assistant is confident about. This can involve inviting the assistant to take a lead in making particular points to the whole class. Teachers say this helps the pupils to see the assistant as a valued member of the team. Of course they have to be careful that this is not seen as an imposition or seen as them delegating what should be their own responsibility. Done well it helps to demonstrate to pupils the value of teamwork. The teachers and assistants are in their actions showing the pupils that it is a positive way of working.

Learning in partnerships

Learning from each other at feedback times not only helps to inform planning, it becomes a form of classroom-based staff development. Discussions that actively seek out what each of the team partners can offer, in the way of understanding what they can both learn and use, are particularly valuable. This might be about pupils and their learning and responses; curriculum approaches; classroom organisation; working together in partnership and learning together about a joint task. There was evidence in many of the researched schools that there was an understanding that 'learning on the job' and with the teachers was one of the most valued aspects of assistants' perceptions of their part in the development of practice.

In a few of the lessons observed, the teacher and assistant discussed with the children how they thought the lesson had gone, in terms of their learning but also the strategies used to support their learning by the two adults. This meant that reflecting on learning took place explicitly with the adults and pupils all involved in the process. 'Remembering to leave time is hard,' said one of the teachers, admitting they didn't always manage it, but saying that it was worthwhile when they did do it. The chapter that follows picks up on learning in partnerships as part of staff development.

Managers' responsibilities

In respect of the identified need for using whatever planning opportunities arose there was evidence in the researched schools that senior managers had recognised that teachers' hours did not always coincide with the working hours of assistants and had tried to rectify this, often in flexible and creative ways. Contracts, flexibility of working hours, and timetabling reorganisation were all areas that had been addressed. Teachers and assistants said that they were only able to be creative in limited ways for themselves and needed senior staff to consider organisational changes in order to establish regular medium- and long-term planning opportunities. They had used their powers of persuasion with school managers in order to make progress.

Senior managers realised that assistants often put too much of their own time into school because of their enthusiasm and were staying in school to plan with teachers at times they were not getting paid to do this. This had led to assistants' hours being extended in some cases or adjusted to make sure that they could meet with teachers at times when the pupils were not in school. Sometimes this meant that the teachers agreed that the assistant was not in class for part of a morning or afternoon, but that the time was better spent planning after school or on a closure day. As one teacher said 'at first I was unsure about managing without her for two lessons, but the planning time we got more than made up for that. When we were together in class we were so much better organised and clear.'

The creative and flexible strategies that had been used differed from school to school and it is not possible to say which is the best way to create planning time. In one example a learning support coordinator was released from class teaching commitments in a primary school in order to plan with a TA, managers seeing the need to fund the cover of the coordinator's class. In some other schools the Senco, who was not on a full teaching timetable, would release teachers on a regular basis so that they could get quality planning time with their assistants. Some use was made of assembly or story time to release pairs of teachers and assistants on a regular basis. The headteacher showed tangible management support in other schools by releasing teachers or coordinators to work with assistants on a regular and 'sacrosanct' basis, by covering their classes themselves.

The learning support coordinator's management role

With respect to the assistants' relationships and working practices in teamwork with the learning support coordinator (Senco), an impressive liaison system was in place in many of the schools. As a part of the coordinator's role in the mentoring and management of assistants, they paid attention to the careful coordination of their work. This task was often difficult to fit into everything that had to be done, for differing reasons in primary and secondary contexts.

In primary contexts the fact that coordinators often have very small amounts of time during the week to carry out activities in support of the assistants can lead to difficulties. A full-time teaching commitment is often the reason. In several of the project schools, where there were several assistants, the school management team had recognised the need for the learning support coordinator to have off-timetable time to meet with, organise and support the assistants. This was done with no extra funding, but with priorities made about existing funds, the managers of the school seeing that the potential of the assistants was unlikely to be fulfilled if there was no key figure working on their behalf in the school. In a primary school with a team of eleven assistants the learning support coordinator, who was also the deputy head, had carefully established a series of meetings with the team. They had begun to discuss questions such as 'How are we feeling about the job?' and 'What could the school do to improve the situation?' each having led to positive actions on the part of the school's leaders, the learning support coordinator providing a direct conduit to them.

In secondary contexts the liaison issues are complex, particularly in respect of the numbers of teaching staff that potentially work with an assistant during the course of the week. Clearly, in these situations it is necessary for the coordinator to have an overview of this work, and to work as an advocate for assistants with heads of subject departments and subject teachers. This had been done in different ways in the researched schools. In two secondary schools a senior assistant had been appointed to support the coordinator in the organisational tasks. The experience of the assistants had been seen as valuable and relevant to the task and they were paid more, from the school's budget, to assist the coordinator in a variety of ways. Their job descriptions had been revised.

In other secondary schools a series of meetings had been called or attended by the coordinator in respect of curriculum areas. In some of these schools a system of faculty attachments had been set up, where heads of department assumed some responsibility for the assistant(s). This entailed working with them and making sure that the subject teachers in the faculty were clear about their role with assistants in their classrooms and within their subjects. The heads of department then made sure that subject materials were made available to the assistants, and they also supported the development of their subject knowledge. The learning support coordinator then provided an overview of the needs of students and assistants.

Faculty links, through representation by a member of each faculty at a regular meeting, for example half-termly, in the learning support department was another way in which assistants were able to meet, plan and work with subject teachers outside the classroom. Often the coordinator would ask the assistants to provide issues for the agenda, making sure that their needs and ideas were familiar to the link teachers. These issues were then taken back to faculty meetings. Both these strategies by coordinators had led to assistants getting to know subject teachers outside the classroom as well as in it.

Assistants were positive about each of these strategies, saying that they could concentrate on areas they were confident in and also wanted to develop. They also said that they liked to meet and plan with teachers outside the classroom, it increased their knowledge of them as people; and the heads of faculties appreciated them more. Teachers said that it gave them opportunities they valued and it made them plan better for assistants' work with them. The learning support coordinators said it eased their task overall to move into this way of working, although the initial stages were not always easy, they were pleased they had stuck with it, and that the outcomes were beneficial for all.

Managing links with others

Supply teachers

Supply teachers and their relationship with assistants in both primary and secondary contexts were seen as an area for scrutiny. Most schools had recognised this as an issue and were attempting to reduce incidences of assistants actually being the ones acting in the supply role. They were thus providing continuity and knowledge of the topics and pupils, in the absence of the usual teacher. The fact that the assistants were the constant presence and valued for that, had to be balanced with the issue of who was actually being paid to carry out the supply role! Some senior managers were attempting to overcome these difficulties by ensuring that internal staff 'on cover' and outside supply staff were made aware of the expectations of them in respect of how much they should reasonably ask assistants to do.

Parents

Moving on to the relationships that assistants had with others there was clear evidence from our findings that the parents of all children, not just those with special needs, had been familiarised with the assistants' roles. During the development of more flexible practices, for example, during the literacy strategy, many more children than before had been supported by assistants. Leaders in schools had recognised that it was important that the parents were fully informed about this. This was so that there should be no confusion because an assistant might have their child in a group. This was part of the development of flexible practice rather than a reflection of either their child's or, indeed, the assistant's abilities.

As the role of TAs has been portrayed, in the press and some journals, as centred specifically on special needs and allocations through statements, parents understandably may have a narrow perception of the kind of work they do. They may well make the assumption about what 'kinds' of children would work with the assistants. We found that this had been addressed in many of the schools that took part in our research. This was done in a variety of ways, such as documentation in the form of school brochures for new parents, at parents' evenings, and in newsletters. These explained the flexible approaches used and how any pupil might at some time work with an assistant.

The work that assistants carry out in support of pupils with significant learning needs also requires close liaison with some parents. Attention had been paid in the schools investigated to how assistants were supported in this. For example they were often involved, particularly at primary level, in writing in parental contact notebooks, using these to exchange essential information, news, progress and requests. They were particularly helpful where pupils experienced language and communication difficulties. The assistants received guidance on how to write appropriately in these communications with parents.

In secondary schools there was evidence of assistants taking a leading role in 'hosting' parents who were visiting the school to discuss their children or at meetings where aspects of the curriculum were being explained. This was often the case where assistants were helping to coordinate particular programmes followed by groups of students that were in addition or as an alternative to their normal programmes of work. Examples of these were vocational courses and Successmaker. In one school the parents had been consulted on the skills that assistants would need to work with their children. 'Understanding what makes teenagers tick' seemed a rather tall order, but understandable! However, given their knowledge of their own children this seems a creative move which draws parents further into a collaborative inclusive approach.

Governors

Governors had also been drawn in through a variety of means. Many of the schools in which we worked had an assistant on the governing body. This representation meant there was an opportunity for governors to become familiar with the assistants' role, their crucial importance in the school, and the need to prioritise decisions about funding in their favour. This might well be, for example, at times when a senior assistant was to be appointed in recognition of long experience, further qualification or taking on additional responsibilities, requiring the pay rise to be associated with this. This had worked in favour of many assistants as governors were drawn into a recognition that making sure the standards fund, for example, was actually spent in support of the people for whom a proportion of it was allocated by right. One of the primary schools investigated had an experienced assistant on the governing body. She regularly reported to the governors verbally and through written representation. The appointment of a senior assistant and the decision to appoint another assistant had been made as a direct result of this collaboration.

Where there was no assistant representation on the governing body the schools ensured clear representation of the assistants' cause through reporting in the head teacher's report or additional documents about their work for information, approval, etc. Another strategy used was inviting a governor to the assistants' meeting(s) or to observe the work of assistants in the classroom.

One of the secondary schools showed evidence of a very coordinated response that involved a joint research interview with the head teacher, chair of governors and learning support coordinator that lasted for over an hour. This demonstrated the school leadership's commitment to the importance of the governors' involvement in and understanding of the work of assistants. This was also, on the evidence of other interviews and classroom observations, the most inclusive school seen. There were three assistants on senior status level and paid appropriately from within school funds. The status of the assistant team in the school was recognised and appreciated by teaching staff. Planning time for assistants and teachers was high on the agenda and there was impressive funding for the staff development of assistants. The governors' involvement was a crucial element in the realisation of these practices.

Working with other professionals

Other professionals who came into school were also connected into the work of assistants in a variety of ways. In the schools we visited these included LEA advisory staff, some of whom had a management function in relation to allocated assistants; therapists, speech and occupational; educational psychologists; social services and welfare personnel. There was evidence in several of the schools that close attention had been paid to this interface. The school managers were careful to make sure that at no point were the assistants put in the position of replacing completely teachers' or managers' contact with any of these personnel, but, nevertheless, there were additional benefits through a careful and supported delegation of the contact/liaison. This might be in relation to the pupils whom assistants knew well or to dissemination to other staff of particular strategies recommended by, for example, the speech therapist.

There was evidence in some schools that close attention had been paid to potential and actual tensions associated with the management of LEA assistants, allocated to schools to support pupils with significant additional needs. The school managers did experience difficulties when the LEA managers or advisory staff were advising assistants to work in ways that ran counter to what was expected within the school's own policy and practice. This meant that the assistants themselves, and sometimes the pupils, were caught in this area of disagreement to the detriment of effective practice. To overcome these problems it was important for school staff to liaise carefully with LEA managers who had responsibility to monitor and support the assistants.

Close and effective liaison was observed between assistants and advisory staff for visual and hearing impairment in two primary schools. It was also seen in a special school, where a senior assistant then provided staff development for her colleagues about the support of visually impaired pupils, after working in her designated 'special area of accountability', in close contact with the LEA and RNIB staff who came to the school.

This chapter has explored the crucial area of team development, in teacher assistant pairs and in wider groups. We have also reviewed managers' roles in supporting this, and the links between assistants and other adults associated with the school. The evidence provided offers real insights into ways the schools we visited had found of addressing these issues. The next chapter goes on to explore team development for assistants themselves and meeting their needs for professional development.

5 Developing assistant teams and reviewing performance and promoting development

This chapter examines the ways in which the schools and services investigated in the Manchester research were facilitating the development of assistant teams and the reasons for and purposes of this. It also considers how the schools and services had addressed the development of effective induction strategies, supported ongoing professional development and the creation of career structures. The schools had also recognised the need for teachers to be supported in their staff development with respect to working effectively with assistants in the classroom and had started to address this. This latter was in the absence of any national and, in most cases, LEA initiatives in this direction at that time.

Despite the lack of opportunities nationally for staff development and training, the professionalism and enthusiasm amongst the assistants we interviewed and observed in class was impressive. This was in part due to the professional regard that their schools, particularly the headteachers and heads of services, had for them and partly due to the positive self-esteem they themselves exhibited. There was also evidence that in these schools there was an understanding on the part of governors, parents and the wider school community about their roles. This was not a coincidence, but was because leaders in the school had taken the decision that it should be so.

Developing the assistant team

In considering the development of assistants through their own team meetings there is a need to be sure that this runs in parallel with teacher/assistant meetings, otherwise a 'them and us' situation might arise. However, as a discrete group in the school or service, they have needs that are distinctly different from those of teachers. Many schools and services we visited created a forum for a variety of purposes. These included: the identification of professional development and training needs; problem-solving around issues raised within the team; the creation of agendas that they wished to raise in the school about their roles and working conditions; induction support for new team members; professional development, from either a guest provider or one of their own number who had attended a course that they wished to share with others; reviewing their personal professional development and developing self-esteem; and inviting a member of the school's management team to raise relevant issues for that group to discuss/act upon.

Examples noted and observed in the schools and services provided real insights into the importance of these meetings. In a special school the assistants shared the key points from courses or staff development meetings they had attended. This was seen as particularly important with respect to skill areas such as lifting; supporting pupils who were deaf/blind; managing extremely challenging behaviour; signing; and understanding autism and its implications. They had also had sessions about curriculum development, particularly in response to using the national literacy strategy in the school. This was mirrored in a primary school where assistants had originally been 'left out' of the first phase of literacy strategy training, an omission that happened in many schools nationally, and they were having 'catch up' sessions, alongside some further sessions with the teaching staff. Given the central role that assistants take in the strategy this was seen as essential. The head of the school said that he would make sure the assistants were 'in the numeracy strategy from the word go'.

In another primary school assistants who had attended courses put together a précis of these and rehearsed with the assistant team ways of doing the same thing for teachers at a whole staff meeting. Advice and guidance was generated in the meeting that would make sharing it with the teachers more effective and relevant.

In a large secondary school with a substantial number of assistants the meetings were used for planning and organisational decision-making about the team's work. This was led by the senior assistant on a weekly basis and entailed delegating responsibility for key members of the team. Teaching staff saw this as essential to the coordination of the assistants' work across the school.

In three LEA services the assistants said how much they valued service team meetings, because although they were allocated to schools and did attend meetings of various kinds in those schools, they felt support for their professional needs were also met through regular team meetings. This was seen as happening in two major ways. One was appropriate support for their skill development in areas such as managing behaviour and encouraging on-task learning. The other was for problem-solving and comparing notes with other assistants allocated to schools who were performing similar roles. They spent some time trying to make sense of how to fit into the schools' varying ethos and organisation, attitudes and practices. It also meant that they felt like a 'team' and had opportunities to meet with their LEA line managers.

Simply getting together with others had helped the assistants to make sense of the job. They were able to support one another. Even experienced assistants found it helped them, particularly in times of altered responsibilities, such as at the start of a new school year. However, these meetings had great significance for new members of the team, particularly where formally they were seen as part of the induction procedures.

Induction procedures

There were some impressive induction procedures in many of the researched schools and services. In several schools the experienced assistants played a large part in this. In one large secondary school, one of the senior assistants' key responsibilities was organising the programmes of induction for new assistants. Job-shadowing programmes, regular short support meetings with the newcomers, staff development meetings with the whole team that were led by other assistants, liaison with senior teaching staff over their part in the programme were all aspects of these responsibilities.

In a primary school where the learning support coordinator had some time off-timetable to coordinate the work of a substantial team of assistants she met new assistants once a week for the first half term of their job. She saw this as vital to their 'settling in' processes, making the point that it was trusting an awful lot to luck in the early days if this was omitted. She said that they could hardly be expected 'to be in-class on child-contact full-time and be effective if they didn't know what the job was about'. She felt it to be an unreasonable demand to make. It also gave an opportunity to underline the commitment they made on appointment to 'grow into the job' and be trained appropriately, as issues that arose highlighted staff development needs in individuals.

Managing staff development opportunities for both assistants and teachers

The issue of playing to assistants' strengths that was examined in Chapter 3 leads to the need to develop these skills and share them through carefully managed staff development opportunities. Where school or service staff development plans target the needs of assistants, this supports their work and responsibilities. In many of the schools we worked in this had been done in conjunction with the staff/professional development review process. Where assistants were encouraged to take up staff development by their mentors and line or senior managers, these managers had identified and allocated funding that was the assistants' entitlement, from the standards fund.

Staff development opportunities might be internally in the school, or on further courses of training, external to the school and through LEA/FE/HE/voluntary organisations. A proportion of the standards fund is TAs' by right, and as such should be used to support their staff development. In schools flexible approaches include job-shadowing, paying assistants to attend school closure days and offering additional pay to attend other in-service sessions. The courses offered in the LEA or by further education colleges often complement opportunities available in school.

However, there seems little point in addressing the needs of assistants if at the same time the managers of the school do not recognise the needs of teachers in support of their skills in the management of assistants in the classroom. It has been the case for many years that neither ITT nor in-service training has addressed the needs of teachers in learning the skills of managing another adult in the classroom. This includes developing partnership working skills and using teaching strategies and classroom management and organisational skills which take account of the presence of an assistant.

In the schools where effective classroom management and teamwork was observed, attention had been paid to the needs of teachers to learn and develop these skills with other teachers and assistants in the school, plugging the gaps through staff development opportunities. In many schools the quality of classroom teamwork has far more to do with teachers having a natural affinity for teamwork, being at ease with an 'open classroom culture' and having a commitment to developing their work in this area.

Many more teachers feel threatened by the assistant's presence – 'Who is she watching and who will she tell?' These teachers often have developed experiences during the 'closed-door culture' era and find it difficult to feel comfortable with an assistant or any other adult in the classroom. Even in the researched schools, during interviews teachers mentioned 'reluctant' colleagues who lacked skills and/or confidence. They were sorry for them – 'They don't know what they're missing!' Their previous experiences and resulting attitude sometimes lead to poor personal dynamics between teachers and assistants and can set up some tense and difficult situations.

Often the children may be the ones who suffer as a result of this tension. What they do not see when this happens is a model of partnership/pair/ team working which will encourage them to be good team members themselves. This lack, in an age of cooperation and skills of citizenship studies, is hardly appropriate. What children also do not experience is a classroom that feels inclusive to assistants, which may be mirrored in their own feelings about themselves too.

Sensitive managers know that the requisite skills do not develop overnight for many teachers and may never develop for some, unless some structured advice and guidance, ideas and strategies are offered to them. Hence the need to recognise the needs of teachers as well as assistants in the school staff development plan and through individual professional development targets for teachers. Managers may well use performance management indicators, which is another strategy in developing teachers' skills in these ways of working. Currently this should not be seen as an optional skill as the increasing numbers of assistants in schools means that more or less all teachers may have to share their classroom at some stage. The researched schools had begun to consider this strategy as an option.

Feedback and learning about classroom practice

Staff development opportunities with small or larger groups of staff may lead to the development of a language of practice around teamwork and classroom partnerships. The detail of how teachers and assistants can plan together, develop their classroom strategies together and monitor how successful they feel their efforts have been, then has the potential to develop into a clear set of procedures. This may be very individual in detail to each partnership, but also may fit into an agreed language of practice and procedures that many staff can use successfully and interchangeably. Learning in partnerships was an important factor in the schools that were observed.

Chapter 4 examined details of that practice in order to illustrate ways in which effective teams could work in the schools observed during the research. Flexibility of deployment through the use of a language of practice was clearly evident in the schools with the most effective ways of working. This had happened because managers, both senior and classroom, had recognised the need for it to happen.

It is, however, helpful to mention here that managers in schools where there was effective practice had also set up a culture of feedback from assistants about their experiences in the classroom. That culture encouraged an openness amongst staff, valuing what assistants had to say about their work with teachers. This might range from seeking their opinion about children's progress, but where there were clearly flexible forms of deployment, feedback extended well beyond this. It included feedback on classroom arrangements, teamwork and partnership. It also included feedback on whether the levels of involvement and understanding of the management of the behaviour policy in the school was sufficient to help assistants to feel confident about playing their part in being consistent in the management of individual pupils or groups of pupils. Finally it included many features of classroom life, and was not just about the work of individual children.

Appraisal and professional development review

The rewriting of job descriptions had led to the development of appraisal systems. Some of the assistants described 'feeling scared the first time', as it was a new experience for many. Interestingly some assistants who had been in other jobs outside education had been in company and service appraisal schemes and were used to the idea. They had reassured others who were nervous, in the early stages.

However, although these processes were in the early stages in many schools, assistants were already saying that they valued the opportunity to be appraised, saying it gave them a sense of 'worth' and made them 'more professional, like the teachers'.

Professional development portfolios

As schools and services had begun to clarify their practices on the roles of TAs and had developed their review and appraisal processes, they had also started to think about tangible evidence of their assistants' achievements. It was early in their moves in this direction but they were beginning to put together portfolios of achievement. They wanted assistants and others to have evidence of skill development, responsibilities that they had taken on, and also courses, conferences, staff development and training sessions they had attended. Where relevant, associated certification was also added. There were two major reasons given for this. It was felt that portfolios would add to professional development review processes of assistants, but also there was anticipation that soon there might be a career structure at a national level and they would have evidence to make a case for their appropriate place in this.

Schools were experimenting with the format that the portfolio should take and how it might be organised. There seemed to be two main ways. One was aligned to the job description structure, with evidence of skills, experiences and training under each of the headings of support for pupils, teachers, curriculum and school. As their evidence was collated any gaps requiring training or other action either by the assistant or other staff in the school was identified. As one assistant said, 'That was really useful. I'd forgotten how much I've done!' A learning support coordinator said, 'If this doesn't prove how much they deserve to be paid more, I don't know what does.'

The other major way of doing this was as a chronological record that looked something like a CV. This way helped to give a clear picture of the personal professional development of the individual concerned. It was not so clear how this aligned to the current job description, with targets for the year in each dimension, and the appraisal procedure, but the process of putting all the evidence together was in itself a valuable one. It also helped to show who had some talents that were perhaps not being used as well as they might within current job descriptions. This was often the case in respect of skills and knowledge brought in from previous employment, but not recognised by the school as useful, for example, in support of the curriculum or partnerships with teachers.

Of course some schools had already created an internal career structure and the portfolio of evidence also supported the assistants' place in this.

Career structures

Most of the assistants interviewed in the research stated clearly that they wanted to be recognised for their roles as assistants not eventually as teachers. They did not see the 'top rung' as qualified teacher status, despite the fact that the DfEE had been speculating that the majority of assistants did want to become teachers. The assistants wanted a top rung and some steps towards that relating to a professional recognition as a valued assistant with impressive experience, skills and qualifications which was reflected in enhanced status and more pay.

In several of the researched schools senior assistants had been appointed and were being recognised for their experience, additional responsibilities, relevant training and qualifications. These developments had occurred despite the absence of a recognised national career structure, but because the school managers had seen it as a priority.

In summary, then, this chapter has explored the nature of effective team and individual professional development for assistants. In the next section of the book the action research strategies using indicators of effective practice within a pilot research project and their outcomes are described. Included are many practical examples of what schools actually did. Chapter 6 starts with an overview of the key strategies that led to successful outcomes.

Section 3
Strategies drawn from experiences in schools and LEAs

The purpose of Section 3 is to provide practical examples of work undertaken by schools and support services that illustrate how, in their different ways, they have developed their work with teaching assistants. The origins of these examples were a series of workshops that examined indicators of effective practice in the work of TAs. In Chapter 6 we describe the process of setting up these workshops and we provide an overview of the range of work and strategies used by the participating schools and support services that took part. Chapters 7 to 12 contain detailed examples of the work that some of the settings undertook, and this is presented under the key headings contained in the Good Practice Guide. Inevitably, there is insufficient space to do justice to all the innovative initiatives that took place and we have therefore chosen examples that illustrate the range of work that was undertaken. Most of these examples have been written with the help of staff in the settings and they are accompanied by copies of actual documents that they produced, either in the main body of the text, in the appendix or on the website, clearly marked with reference to chapters and page numbers.

The whole process of initiating and running the workshops and supporting the schools and support services in their follow-up work reflected an action research approach to development work in each of the settings. In this sense the strategies they undertook were continually scrutinised, evaluated and revised by the staff involved. This process is reflected in some of the examples we have given in that we sometimes present initial and revised action research plans to illustrate how the work progressed together with an analysis of why the participants chose to work in this way.

6 Strategies that support the development activities

This chapter describes the process of setting up the workshops that were the initial starting points for the action research project. This is followed with a summary of the activities in which the participating schools and support services engaged.

The structure of the action research project

Chapter 2 refers to the conclusions of the Manchester research in which we defined effective practice in the work of assistants as involving contributions that:

- foster the *participation* of pupils in the social and academic processes of a school;
- seek to enable pupils to become more *independent* learners;
- help to *raise standards* for all pupils.

These key features have been adopted in the Good Practice Guide (GPG). Our report also contained a set of more detailed indicators of effective practice (see Chapter 2) that were intended to be used as a development tool for staff in schools and support services to stimulate development in the work of assistants. The overall aim of the action research project was to pilot the use of the indicators and review questions through working directly with staff in schools and support services in different LEAs. In this way we could see at first hand how effective this strategy could be in bringing about improvements in the work of TAs.

In setting up the pilot action research project we were keen to work with a variety of LEAs and schools. This enabled us to explore the impact of the approach in varied settings so as to ensure that their work was subjected to rigorous scrutiny and to help us obtain a picture of whether the indicators and review questions could be applied in settings that were geographically, demographically and organisationally different.

We chose to work with schools and support services in three LEAs, Cheshire, Harrow and Salford. Within each LEA there were four 'sites' that reflected different phases and ages of pupils, some of which had additional provision, for example for pupils with physical disabilities, and some were LEA support services. The criteria in the choice of representatives from each of these sites were that one should be a senior member of the teaching staff, preferably from the senior management team, and one or more should be an assistant. A full list of participants and short description of each setting is provided in Appendix 1.

The first phase of the original action research plan drawn up in consultation with the participants consisted of the following steps.

1. An initial workshop in each of the three LEAs for the participants from each of the four sites. This was also attended by a senior officer from the LEA.
2. Ongoing development work in the schools/services.
3. A visit from one of the authors (Balshaw) to each of the schools/services.
4. The presentation of a draft report to an evaluation conference.

This was followed by a second phase that included the following:

1. further meetings within the LEA groups;
2. gathering data to inform the writing of the DfES Good Practice Guide;
3. negotiations over the writing of this book;
4. reporting the research to wider audiences in LEAs and nationally (the key to this were the DfES dissemination conferences on the GPG at which schools and services made presentations of their action research project work).

(See Appendix 2 for a detailed outline of the original research plan.)

At the initial workshops in the first phase participants were familiarised with the contents of the Manchester research report through presentations, discussions and activities. They made some preliminary choices of the indicators (see Appendix 3) and review questions that they felt would support their practice and development in schools. Firstly, for discussion purposes edited versions of these were used both to facilitate understanding and to stimulate ideas (see Appendix 4, which provides versions of these edited sets of questions using the GPG text, instead of the Manchester version used in the workshop).

Although there was a spread of choices made in the twelve sites (in the three LEAs) – see Appendix 3 – those chosen by participants from most settings were in the *management dimension*. Nine sites worked on these in some detail to consider what their management practice was at the outset and how it might be developed. Significantly, the indicator chosen by seven of these was indicator B2 (*Schools have policies outlining roles and responsibilities of LSAs*). This points to their perceived need to focus on the management structures of the schools/services themselves and their impact on the assistants in their teams.

A key stage in setting up the project in each LEA was the introductory workshop. Indeed, in the participants' evaluation emphasis was placed on its importance for the research coordinators themselves. This was in relation to developing their understanding of the issues, how these related to their own context, exploring potential strategies and their confidence in carrying out the work. In addition, the workshops provided the opportunity to make an initial assessment of the indicators and review questions which they provisionally chose to use, in further consultation with other colleagues in their own context.

A draft action research plan was drawn up at these initial workshops and discussed with other participants so that strategic ideas were pooled amongst the participants. Clearly, in carrying out action research in individual settings, this kind of workshop session, held in context, for a school's key coordination team (or 'lead researchers') forms a key plank of the strategy. This should involve using the Good Practice Guide indicators and questions, similar to the way the pilot participants used the Manchester University indicators. Figure 6.1 provides a suggested format for a strategic plan in order to undertake this work.

Action research plans

The action research plans drawn up by the individual schools and support services varied in content and in this way met the needs of the differing sites. In the main they covered the timescale of two terms initially, but there were sections outlining longer-term ambitions. Many of them started off with a data-gathering period, using the indicators chosen at the initial workshop as a means of providing a focus. However, many also made plans to involve other key people from their settings in the days immediately after the workshop. There are some examples in Appendix 5.

Broadly, the strategies used consisted of two types:

1. Using existing structures, such as meetings, timetabled sessions, staff development activities, forums for dissemination and management structures, documentation, etc., in order to gather information, analyse data and draw up strategic plans.
2. Developing additional activities, strategies and structures to enable both data collection and development work.

In most cases, however, there was a combination of these two approaches. For example, in one high school, it was found that, where representations had already been made *on behalf of* assistants at senior management meetings, this was changed to their *actual participation* in these meetings. They attended in order to inject the priorities and ideas identified by the key team, in order to develop awareness and seek practical management support with the activation of these. Each of these strategies was used in the following ways:

1. Using existing structures

These activities all happened in at least two contexts and in some cases more:

- Building on already existing structure of professional development meetings for assistants.
- New/revised timelines for team meetings of assistants (mostly with assistants/learning support coordinator or heads of service).

This is a suggested format for creating the contextual conditions in order to
- **draw up an action research plan using the Good Practice Guide**
- **involve key people as 'lead researchers' and others in gathering data and moving practice forward**

This needs to be 'loose enough' to work in any context and encourage flexibility and creativity whilst also providing a strong framework for supporting the action research at a strategic and practical level.

<u>**Preparing the context**</u>

Senior management and governors should be clear about
- the need for the action research to happen and why
- their respective roles in supporting the development work

A key group of people comprising **at least one senior manager and two assistants (lead researchers)** should be identified and meet with the management team for an exploratory/focused discussion about the purposes of the research work. A working knowledge of the GPG should be developed through this group activity.

<u>**Carrying out a preliminary audit/review**</u>

The lead researchers should make some decisions about potential areas to be addressed through carrying out a review themselves using **the GPG indicators and review questions.** These ideas should be discussed with senior managers and agreed as the school/service's areas of focus for gathering further information/data.

<u>**Drawing up a research plan for gathering further data and taking action**</u>

This should cover the immediate, the next few weeks and also some longer-term goals. It should contain two major elements: data collection processes and developments in practice.

<u>**Questions to ask:**</u>
- Which **indicators** and **review questions shall we use?**
- Who should we ask to find the information/data we need (pupils, parents, assistants, governors, senior staff, class teachers, heads of departments, LEA staff)
- **When and how** will we do this?
- Which meeting might be the best forum? Will it go on an **existing agenda**/fit into **an existing structure** or plan? Are there already **timetabled opportunities** we can use?
- What **additional strategies**/activities might we need to use (e.g. extra meetings/different groupings from the 'usual' ones/questionnaire or interviews)?
- What **potential barriers** do we see and how will we deal with them?
- What **outcomes** do we anticipate?

<u>**The research action plan format**</u>

Suggested data gathering/activities framework to complete:

Task/indicator focus	By whom	How	By when	Outcomes

<u>**Evaluating outcomes**</u>

These might be associated with two major strands:
- **data collection/useful information** that has led to increased understanding of the issues associated with the focus identified by the choice of indicator
- **development activities** and changes in:
  classroom practice and role, planning and partnership developments (teachers/TAs)
  staff development practices and training
  policy and practice development at management level

Identify **success criteria.**

These may be about:
- the quality/usefulness of data/information and/or
- actions taken on the strength of that information and/or
- about developments in practice and policies.

Figure 6.1 A strategic plan

- Focused/refocused planning time (e.g. identifying 'protected' time, using it well).
- Representation at senior management team meetings.

2. Additional activities

The following strategies were used in several settings. Specifically, questionnaires were devised in seven sites that were based on the indicator and review question process (there are examples in Appendix 6 of some of them, clearly showing their origins in these questions):

- Questionnaires based on the chosen indicators/research questions, reflecting the focus selected for review and development (sometimes simultaneously to teachers and assistants/sometimes in stages to elicit follow-up data or different perspectives on earlier data, in some contexts including parents and pupils).
- Reporting back to and meeting with key individuals (e.g. learning support coordinator, deputy head, headteacher, senior management team).
- Involving parents and children in discussions and in seeking data.
- Open forum with all staff (e.g. for discussions of the issues identified/ brainstorming ideas).
- Representations/participation in senior management team meetings.

In addition to these two broad strategies, the following specific approaches were used in individual settings:

- Flow chart analysis of the TA role based on typical day/week
- Targeting for review and development work with specific departments and/or children
- Job shadowing for gathering data/information
- Analysing existing job descriptions and discussing information found
- Swapping roles to learn about one another's work
- Professional development interviews
- Interviews with children
- Ongoing discussions with school governors
- Newsletters to schools about work of the support service

It seems very clear from this evidence that the use of the indicators and review questions had stimulated a great deal of creativity in devising methodologies for both gathering information and developing new ways of working. The range of techniques used of course reflects very differing contexts, but there was a clear demonstration of the flexibility of choosing appropriate indicators and the questions associated with them. Moreover, the adaptation of the questions to suit a context, for example, changing the wording or adding wholly new questions, means that participants and their schools/services saw their potential as a means to bring about change. Some examples of these appear in later chapters.

Potential barriers

It is important to acknowledge that the participants encountered some barriers/problems in the course of their work. These included:

- General difficulties over time availability in schools, where the ongoing agendas were competing with the project work.
- The coordination of project meetings within existing timetabling constraints.
- Initial anxieties over drawing in more closely governors and parents in the analysis of assistants' roles.
- Initial anxieties over teachers' perceptions of the initiative, perhaps that they might feel threatened, or that it might be seen as creating extra work for them.

It seems important to recognise that there are potential barriers to the development work in any context. Apart from the specific examples given above there are others. Amongst these may be: existing attitudes about the 'place' and role of assistants in the school; pressures from multiple innovations; a lack of recognition by senior staff about the importance of the work; the reluctance of assistants to see their role in carrying out research. However, where any of these factors exists the presence of a carefully chosen lead research team can make a real difference in the ability to break down the barriers. A problem-solving culture can be developed within the small team and shared with other colleagues in order to overcome any difficulties encountered.

Outcomes

There is no doubt that a significant impact was made in all of the twelve settings that took part in the action research project. This was in both the plans made for the initial period of five terms and also the new academic year beginning in September 2001. Clearly, the role of assistants was examined very closely in the sites, through a focus on job descriptions and management practices, with staff development opportunities and induction processes also receiving in-depth attention. Management issues were paramount in the majority of settings and some significant strides were made in developing awareness of issues identified within the indicators of effective practice, leading to changes in management practices. This in turn led to developments in both policy and practice.

What is also worthy of comment is the fact that having a senior member of staff strategically to fulfil a leadership and advocacy role was a key to success. Without this person to keep the 'voice' of the action researchers on agendas and in discussions with key groups of people such as senior managers or governors there would have been much more potential for the projects to lose focus and/or momentum. However, having said that, the self-advocacy generated by both the lead researcher assistants and the whole teams of assistants has placed them firmly at the forefront of staff development and school improvement in many settings. The lead that assistants took at the national dissemination conferences was impressive, their appreciative audiences applauding them and their presentations, their confidence and their work. Readers will be impressed with the accounts of the development of confidence and self-esteem that came from their involvement in action research. They are rightly proud of these achievements.

In recommending the use of indicators of effective practice the researchers (both participant researchers and university researchers) feel confident that the lessons learnt within this project are likely to be useful to others contemplating a review and development of new initiatives in their own schools and services. The particular issue of effective strategies in carrying out the action research has therefore led to the advice and guidance, ideas and materials that are included in this book. These lessons should transfer comfortably in order to support the use of the revised version of the indicators that form part of the DfES's Good Practice Guide, *Working with Teaching Assistants*.

The six chapters that now follow each focus on one of the six management areas identified within the Good Practice Guide. These are: roles and responsibilities; flexibility of deployment; partnerships between teachers and TAs; working with others in education; team development for TAs and professional development.

7 Developing clear job descriptions and accountabilities

The exploration of the issues in Chapter 3 can now be illustrated with practical examples drawn from the schools and LEAs that carried out the action research based on the use of indicators and review questions. It was significant that in the first review of practice carried out by the participants at the first workshop the majority (7/12) chose to scrutinise the status of their current TA job descriptions. The process of reflecting on the indicator about management policy and the associated review questions that asked about 'up-to-date and relevant job descriptions' and whether these had been 'drawn up with the assistants' involvement' and 'reviewed on a regular basis' prompted them to take immediate action. Interestingly, other schools, although not starting with this focus, also moved on to this area realising that it was an aspect that should be addressed.

The participants were aware that the current sets of job descriptions were in many cases out of date, describing a more rigid and traditional set of responsibilities that did not reflect the way in which the role had developed and changed in recent times. Moreover, in two situations there was doubt about whether there was a school job description at all, the only existing document being an outline one issued by the LEA.

On returning to school to consider the questions that might be addressed in conjunction with other colleagues and particularly the other assistants in the team, there were different action research strategies drawn up in each context. Examples of these are to be found in the previous chapter and Appendix 5, and on the website, each with activities and timeline reflecting the contextual needs.

In **Ryles Park High School, Cheshire**, after the workshop review, the assistants Carolyn and Sam, and the Senco, Rosemary, met with all the support team to consider the review questions selected by these lead researchers as a focus. Rosemary also enlisted the support of the deputy head, John, who provided invaluable senior management team support in a variety of ways, both moral and practical, and he indicated a clear commitment to how important he felt the work was. A decision was made to revise and rewrite the job descriptions as a group and individually in such a way that they reflected current responsibilities. They were aware that, as they had already started to work in curriculum support attached to faculties, they needed, in particular, to add the 'curriculum dimension' to their existing accountabilities. Along with the addition of this dimension they completely regrouped and revised the relevant existing responsibilities so that they fitted the four-dimensional outline suggested in the GPG. The team did this with the active and involved support of the deputy head, who acknowledged that it was important to address these issues. The following is the first page of Carolyn's job description, the full version is in Appendix 7, with another example on the website.

Job Description

Name: Carolyn Ashcroft
Job Title: Teaching Assistant
Grade:
Hours P/W: 32.5 hours per week
School: Ryles Park High School, Macclesfield
Accountable to:

Job Purpose: To enhance the learning of pupils who have a wide range of learning needs; by supporting the teaching staff in enabling the pupils to gain independence and participate fully in the curriculum and general life of the school. To be adaptable, have empathy but also follow the school's 'positive discipline' guidelines.

Duties and Responsibilities
Support for the pupil
Central to the whole principle of inclusion – those children who have learning or physical difficulties should be helped to work independently in the company of other children across the curriculum.

Support for the teachers
To develop a mutually supportive relationship with all teaching staff. Endeavour to help pupils gain access to the curriculum by differentiating instructions and resources. Assisting pupils to become better learners by discreetly prompting them to stay 'on task'.

Support for the curriculum
Support the delivery of the Literacy and Mathematics strategy along with other aspects of both the National Curriculum and the enhanced curriculum offered by school.

Support for the school
To work as part of a flexible and supportive team to further the ethos of the school. To undertake relevant training to enhance personal development and to use the knowledge to benefit the school. To attend $^1/_2$ termly TA meetings to develop and disseminate good practice.

Key accountabilities:
• The management and administration of SuccessMaker. Duties include: enrolling pupils, monitoring their individual progress, designing and producing certificates which acknowledge their effort and progress, ensuring the smooth running of the programme, generating reports and homework throughout the school year, and contact with parents.

• To continue as the link liaison person within the mathematics department by attending all relevant meetings, held both in and out of school. This role also includes involvement in the mathematics pilot scheme.

As can be seen from these examples the nature of the four dimensions of the role is clearly defined, but what is also evident is that individuals' particular strengths and interests are clear, so each set of accountabilities is personalised to the individual concerned. At the point later, where professional development reviews take place, close reference can be made to these in respect of appraisal and the identification of success criteria in terms of the individual's particular skills and accountabilities and their fulfilment. The staff development needs of individuals is also made explicit at this stage within the revised framework. This area is dealt with in more detail in Chapter 12.

In **Salford**, the **Moorside High School** research team also decided, during their use of the indicators and review questions in the initial workshop, that a close scrutiny of somewhat outdated job descriptions should take place. This was in relation to the fact that the assistants' roles had developed considerably over the last few years, including their work on faculty links, and the appointment of a senior assistant from within their ranks. This senior assistant, Marie, a colleague, Yvonne, and the deputy head, Dave, comprised the lead research team, who took their ideas to the next departmental meeting. They were also concerned with the 'image of the base' and felt that a clarification of roles and responsibilities would be helpful to the teaching staff, given the developments in practice of the learning support base itself. This led to the assistants also producing 'publicity material' for the base for a variety of uses in the school. Flexibility of deployment was a key feature of this revision of practice, and some more detail of this work appears in Chapter 8.

The job descriptions were revised, taking account of the flexible ways of working that had already developed, but they were also structured into the four dimensions suggested in the Good Practice Guide. Therefore, there was a move from three areas described in the following order, on an old job description:

> The caring role; the educational role, designed to free teachers from some of the more mundane daily tasks; and the paraprofessional role, which centres on developing relevant educational programmes under the guidance of the teacher,

to that of the four areas of support for *pupils*, for *teachers*, for the *curriculum* and for the *school*. The senior assistant's accountabilities were also set out more explicitly than they had been previously.

At present these are all in draft form for a period which will then lead to further review, probably at a time when the national competencies become available and grades of employment may be taken into account within this framework. The redraft of the additional responsibilities carried out by the senior assistant, Marie, below shows how her coordination role is essential to the smooth running of the team.

Primary schools also undertook to research their job descriptions and accountabilities. **Vaughan First and Middle School in Harrow** convened a meeting of all the assistants who worked in the school. The lead researchers, two assistants, Surinder and Jackie, and the deputy head and Senco, Sue, proposed that the team discussed the issues they had identified at their

---

MOORSIDE HIGH

SENIOR TEACHING ASSISTANT JOB DESCRIPTION

1. To fulfil the requirements of the job description relating to a Teaching Assistant.
2. To direct the work of the Teaching Assistants on a day to day basis, putting together appropriate timetables in consultation with the Learning Support Co-ordinator.
3. To chair the weekly staff meeting of the Teaching Assistants.
4. To be present at meetings which involve the Co-ordinator of Learning Support, in order to take minutes, e.g. reviews, parental meetings, etc.
5. To assist the Co-ordinator of Learning Support in the production and maintenance of the necessary administrative systems to sustain the work of the faculty.

---

preliminary review during the workshop. The outcome of this meeting was a 'brainstorming' session involving everyone. Everyone contributed their ideas about what ought to be on the job description from their own personal experiences of doing the job. In this way they generated a much more accurate list, drawn from existing experiences in the school, which actually reflected the ways in which they and their roles had developed in recent times.

Discussions ensued about the accountabilities and duties identified in this activity. An analysis of the data generated led to redefinitions using the four dimensions in the Good Practice Guide. Draft job descriptions were drawn up from the outcomes of this activity and put up for initial agreement by the senior management for a trial period to see if they were appropriate. There was a commitment to review them after an initial period, and make revisions where necessary. The assistants' comments on the website illustrate how they carried out these activities and also how they felt about the project work supporting them in these developments.

At **Parkes Field in Salford** lead researchers, the assistant head, Lynn, and two assistants, Angela and Jane, identified the need to look at the current job descriptions in the workshop review of practice. Following this, at the next meeting of the support staff when there were discussions about the review within the whole team, it was decided to completely redraft the job descriptions. These had been in place for some time but the assistants said they didn't really reflect what they were currently doing, having changed and developed in their roles over a period of time. There was another reason for taking this decision. The school-site was due to close in September 2001 and become part of a purpose-built campus comprising three existing schools. There was a feeling that clarifying roles would be helpful as people were applying for the posts on the new campus and that their work might provide an effective example to be adopted, possibly, within the new school, that assistants from the other two schools might find professionally supportive. Angela, a very experienced assistant, also felt she needed a clear definition of what her more senior role might look like, and she was later appointed as senior assistant in the new school.

Over a series of the regular team meetings the whole team, led by the lead researchers, who were joined in the research team by another assistant, Tinah, worked on the redraft. They submitted their ideas to the headteacher, Anthea, who had provided excellent support through offering extra time to work together and technical back-up from the office. Currently these job descriptions are being piloted and reviewed and will be reconsidered as the three schools become one, Springwood. The headteacher of Parkes Field is to be the head at the new school, the assistant head is to be an assistant head there too. The assistants also all have new posts there, so there is an expectation that the development work will continue, using similar strategies as soon as a period of settling in has taken place. Parkes Field has also done a great deal of work, linked into the roles and responsibilities review on professional development and records of achievement for assistants, which is detailed in Chapter 12 of this book.

In Appendix 7, the 2001 job description shows how the organisation of the revised version is led by different headings, reflecting the structure proposed in the Good Practice Guide.

A team of assistants from **an infants school, Puss Bank, in Cheshire**, reflected on their current job descriptions after the initial workshop. During this workshop review the lead researchers, assistant, Maggi, and learning support coordinator, Catherine, had identified this as one of the areas that they thought should be considered by the whole team of assistants. It was felt that the existing job description in school no longer reflected the changing role of teaching assistants in general or the diverse nature of the role within Puss Bank School. In discussion with the team it was decided that the revisions should establish a core set of roles and responsibilities for all teaching assistants with some individualised components to reflect specific roles of staff within the nursery, special needs department and mainstream school. Attendance by assistants from the school on the DfES programme of induction training for newly appointed TAs had also stimulated this discussion and supported the developments in the school.

The team also wished to introduce a system of professional development review, directly connected into accountabilities. The school team had been thinking of doing this for some time, but was seeking a clear mechanism through which to do it. The indicators and review questions, together with the school's involvement in the 'Investor in People' programme, were making this connection in a way they felt they could use. Details of their professional development review activities are to be found in Chapter 12.

It is possible to trace the development of the job descriptions using a version from 1999 and the most recent one, reflecting the four dimensions recommended in the Good Practice Guide. These appear on the website.

Across the town **Upton Priory Junior School** had three staff at the research workshop and they considered the indicators and review questions. Circumstances in the school led the two assistants, Karen, a senior assistant, and Kath, and Ann, the Senco, to identify a need to reflect with the team of assistants about their current job descriptions, which they were clear were not appropriate. Their school has additional provision for children with physical disabilities and this meant there is a substantial group of assistants dedicated to this work; in addition there are assistants with a more general role. The similarities, overlap in practice and clear individual accountabilities were not explicit enough. The perceptions of the teaching staff about their roles were unclear at times, and the clarification of these was a specific focus for their work.

They got together at a special team meeting (they currently did not have a whole team regular meeting, more about this later in Chapter 11), sanctioned by the headteacher and negotiated at a staff meeting with the teachers. A number of the teachers were a little reluctant, feeling that they couldn't 'manage without' their assistants. However, as a 'one-off' they agreed. Later, of course, further meetings were needed to carry out the action research plan, so some tact was needed on behalf of all to ensure that these could take place.

The outcomes of the ensuing discussions were very positive and their activities, brainstorming what they all did, raised a number of further issues that they felt should be addressed sooner or later. From their discussion of the job description there was an implication about their contracts and the LEA's perspectives and practice. It was agreed that this should be raised with the officers concerned. These further issues in school included the need to establish regular meetings, to help teachers to understand the need and also to take on the revised sets of accountabilities. The head was positive about their ideas and urged patience about taking suitable time to attempt to do all this.

The job descriptions themselves were restructured into the four dimensions of support for the teachers, pupils, curriculum and the school. Clear definition was made in respect of individuals' particular responsibilities. Drafts were drawn up and there was a consultation with the senior management team of the school about them. Currently they are being used in draft form and are under review in the new school year of 2001–2. Teachers are being familiarised with them, and new staff in September 2001 introduced to them in order to facilitate consistency in practice.

Two Harrow schools, Whitmore High and Grange First, took very different courses of action with respect to refining roles and responsibilities. The assistant, Sharon, and Lynne, the deputy head, from **Grange First,** spent much time during the workshop considering the indicator and questions on roles and responsibilities. They thought they should attempt to canvass opinion amongst the whole staff about their perceptions of the assistants' role in the school. There were existing misperceptions and some outdated ideas about the role of assistants on the part of a significant number of teachers, and the wish to develop more flexible ways of working was seen as essential to the development of more inclusive practice in the school. There had been a 'tendency to the underdevelopment of reflective practice'. In part, the decision was also due to some staff changes, and additional support staff having been appointed, which the managers believed should be deployed more flexibly than before. Lynne and the headteacher, Sue, saw a starting point for change here. Their key question was,

How are teachers supporting assistants in working effectively with children?

They decided to devise questionnaires, largely based on the review questions associated with the indicator on role definition, but with specific related questions that probed the Grange context. They drew up one for the assistants and another for the teachers to attempt to gather evidence about where the school currently stood. They also, in their research action plan, made dates at staff and team meetings to both introduce the questionnaires and explain the reasons for doing this. There were then further meetings to debrief the analysis of the data collected, and the implications for both teachers and assistants in their respective roles in the classroom. One of the outcomes was the importance of considering the teachers' needs in developing their practice in planning and working with assistants. Some staff meetings were allocated in which to carry out staff development with teachers and assistants together. Chapter 9 describes these in detail.

There is an example below of the questionnaire to assistants, and on the website there is a compilation of the responses made by the assistants and the questionnaire for teachers.

The outcomes of this have led to a clarification of activities, but crucially some moves forward in terms of classroom practice in respect of the assistants' roles. Moreover some developments in the nature of teacher/assistant partnerships with respect to curriculum approaches have resulted and are ongoing. There is also progress with the assistants' team meetings and professional development, all of which is detailed in later chapters.

Briefly, returning to **Moorside High School in Salford**, in the research team's work on the roles and responsibilities indicator, they also recognised a need to establish a sense of what the teaching staff, students and parents perceived as the role of assistants in the school. The research team drew up three questionnaires for each of these sets of people using the appropriate review questions identified in the initial workshop with the language modified to suit their recipients and also the Moorside context. Over a period of three terms they revised them, piloted them and then distributed them to a sample of each group. They then analysed the messages to be found within them and this has now set them their development agenda during the coming school year.

Some of the responses were 'surprises' that caused the research team to challenge their assumptions. For example, one member of staff suggested that the assistants might benefit from copies of the schemes of work. This had been suggested at the faculty link meetings in the learning support base, and the base staff felt this was happening already, so there had been a breakdown of the system somewhere. Other comments, such as one in response to the question 'What benefits do you gain from the assistants' presence?' helped the assistants to feel valued: 'Vast benefits, could not do without them', which may not have been made at all if an enquiry had not been conducted. Some further descriptions of these research activities can be found in Chapters 8 and 10.

There are examples on the website showing the first draft of the teachers' questionnaire, and clear links to the indicator questions can be made, though it has been drawn up to explore the Moorside context, so there are alterations and additions. Eliciting teachers' perceptions of the Learning Support Base's purpose, from where the assistants' work is directed, is an example of this. There are examples of responses also on the website, using the finalised version.

GRANGE FIRST

THE EFFECTIVE USE OF TEACHING ASSISTANTS' TIME
TEACHING ASSISTANTS' QUESTIONNAIRE

This questionnaire is designed to give you an opportunity to share with us your thoughts and feelings. It is part of our ongoing work to continue to ensure a consistent, supportive and effective use of your time. Please fill in a questionnaire for each teacher you work with. You do not need to name the teacher or to identify yourself.

1 Have you got a job description?	Yes/No
2 Do you find your job description helpful?	Yes/No
3 If yes in what ways?	
4 Have you ever had an opportunity to review your job description?	Yes/No
5 Do you have an opportunity to take part in the planning of lessons?	Yes/No/Sometimes
6 Do you contribute to record keeping?	Yes/No
Are the teacher's expectations of you realistic?	Yes/No/Sometimes
Please comment if you wish	
7 Do you feel your contribution in the classroom is valued?	Yes/No/Sometimes
8 Do you feel you have enough time to do all you are asked in a session (consider preparation, resources and tidying up)?	Yes/No/Sometimes
9 Do you feel you get enough training for your role?	Yes/No
10 Are you interested in further professional development?	Yes/No

Thank you for your time and for the high quality support you provide.
We hope that you feel valued as a member of our school team.

Meanwhile, at **Whitmore High School in Harrow** the research team of assistants, an EMAS teacher working with the learning support department and a governor have been equally diligent. At the workshop Anne and Sneha, assistants, Karen, a teacher, and Angie the governor, considered the indicator and questions with respect to roles and responsibilities. They thought that there was a need to redefine these with the senior management of the school and, through that, the teaching staff and governors. The school rightly has a reputation for effective practice in the special needs field and its inclusive orientation, taking substantial numbers of students with significant additional needs on roll. However, the team felt that there might be a sense of 'staleness', a need for refreshment, and also the need to bring more recent members of staff more closely into the task. The fact that Angie, as a governor, was in the lead team meant that this lent 'weight' to their endeavours, and could reach parts of the system that needed to be reached!

The resulting ongoing developments were in fact in four major areas. The senior management teamwork, and representation at senior management board, is ongoing. In addition there have been developments in respect to: criteria for recruiting new assistants; information for staff about the role of the assistants; faculty attachments work; planning and teacher partnership developments; and partnership with governors and parents. The last four of these are described in Chapters 8, 9 and 10. The assistants have secured in-person representation on the school's management board, where previously their views were represented through the Senco, Janice, but lacked the personal feelings of the assistants. At the first meeting that an assistant attended the head of the school, Peter, was clearly very impressed with their views, ideas and plans, promising positive support in a number of ways, particularly as far as management board was concerned. Peter, together with senior staff and governors felt that, given the large number and distinct nature of the work of the assistants, it was important that they should have their own representation on the school's management board. This meant that there will be continuous attention paid to their overall role and their contacts with senior staff who could get things done on their behalf, for example in respect of faculty attachments. Some of the assistants also went to talk to the senior management team. Anne's recollections of the first two meetings of the board are recorded on the website.

Having taken part in recruitment interviews in her governor role, Angie noted that the recruitment interview agenda contained questions pertinent to the project. A key one was that about which subjects assistants are interested in, confident about, or might like to be attached to, and areas to avoid when timetabling. With the development of the research project this question had an additional purpose. It led to the appointment of assistants who came to the school knowing that this was now a requirement of the developing flexibility in the role. It would open up further possibilities for faculty attachments in the new school year as the trial faculty attachment work in geography and maths was evaluated and expanded into other curriculum areas. This in itself was a clear policy development that was evidence of a commitment to develop more flexible forms of deployment and to think about effective curriculum support, an important dimension of the assistants' job description.

Salford LEA's Primary Partnership Centre was represented at the initial workshop by Sarah and Linda, two support assistants, and Yvette, acting teacher-in-charge. Salford's support service was due for major reorganisation in summer 2000, so staff at the Centre were looking at the indicators that might help them with this, in reference to policy developments and clarification of role. This was particularly with respect to flexibility of deployment, and teamwork with other organisations – the schools they served; medical, psychiatric and social services with whom they liaised over vulnerable pupils was one area they decided they should clarify. This, at a time when they were in for considerable upheaval, possible moves of job and the redefinition of SEN/Behaviour Support Service.

It has been difficult to maintain high levels of activity during a period of major change, but they did spend time, as a whole team, analysing where they were at in respect of many of the review questions, and despite the upheaval through which they have been there have been some positive outcomes. One has been to consider role definitions in the newly formed Primary Partnership Service with Brenda, the manager of support in schools. This has been used to facilitate the assistants' work, particularly in their partnerships with schools where pupils are returning to part- or full-time attendance and the respective roles of receiving teachers, their schools and the service assistants. In later chapters some developments in more flexible deployment, and their partnership work with other teams of professionals, are described.

At **Park Lane School in Cheshire**, Pat, an experienced assistant, and Helen, the assistant head, were also working on some targets for developing clarity of roles. The special school is experienced in managing the work of assistants; nevertheless their review using the indicators and questions during the initial workshop threw into focus some areas that they thought merited attention. A number of new staff, and the fact that there were more assistants than teachers overall, made them think carefully about their respective perceptions of how assistants worked, particularly in relation to the ways they encouraged pupils' independent learning, and how teachers managed this. Questionnaires based on the review questions and indicators, but with specific Park Lane contextual questions added, were drawn up. The assistants' version was given out, some analysis resulted and the teachers' version followed. A result of that has been at a policy level that targets for role accountability have now been defined for individuals. This is currently under review, involving the headteacher, Dave, who has provided support throughout their work, making sure staff meeting agendas accommodated their activities.

These examples from schools and services are all directly related to the indicator and review questions about assistants' roles and responsibilities, teachers' and others' understanding of these and the assistants' role in drawing them up. Of course, some of the ideas initially explored here and the activities described move into other areas and different aspects of the Good Practice Guide. Already there have been activities connected into working more effectively in partnership with teachers and also drawing parents into the research and development agenda. These will be explored in much more detail in later chapters. The next chapter, however, goes on to describe and analyse what some of the schools and services did about flexibility of deployment.

8 Working flexibly with assistants

Following the accounts of how the schools and settings that took part in the research had developed their understandings of roles and responsibilities, this chapter will revisit some of the contexts to investigate what happened as they attempted to develop more flexible strategies for the deployment of assistants. Many of them had already taken considerable steps in this direction but the indicators and review questions dealing with this brought a clearer focus to these steps and suggested further ways forward. The conceptual frameworks explored in Chapter 3 dealt with these issues in respect of the original research and what was learned from it.

The **Harrow Visual Impairment Service** team, on reviewing their practice in the light of the indicators and review questions, felt that they needed to think analytically and strategically how assistants could work more flexibly. They were confident in much of their practice and appreciated by the primary and secondary schools who received support for their pupils. The lead researchers, Janice, Rosie, Jaquie, Kathryn and Margaret, all assistants, and the VI team leader, Elizabeth, realised they should meet to compare what they each did in order to respond flexibly to the needs of the pupils and schools they each supported. Working with different people in a variety of contexts had led to a range of responses that they thought should be shared in a team meeting to see if they could identify some key themes. They also sought to identify the most effective strategies being used by the team members and what of these might be shared. As the team manager, Elizabeth felt this would be an important step in the team's professional development.

They decided to collect data by each carrying out a careful record and analysis of a typical week's work and arranged another team meeting to discuss their findings and the next steps they might take. Their investigations were, as they said, very revealing and their discussions were fruitful. These led them to think in great detail about their planning processes and the ways this was done with the teaching colleagues who had responsibility for the pupils they supported for almost all of the school week.

The team had already established a set of ground rules with schools that emphasised that the pupils' teachers were responsible for the pupils' learning. Thus, the support that was provided was to enable them to work effectively in optimising access to the curriculum at all times, and certainly when there was no additional help to hand. They directly supported pupils less and less, wary of building in dependency, preferring to make sure that they were gaining curriculum access because their teachers were well-informed and skilled at what to do.

What came from their team research was a greater understanding of the range of strategies they used, both individually and collectively. In this way more flexible forms of deployment spread to the whole team. As team leader Elizabeth became much more aware of what each of her team were doing and also of the value of meeting more regularly as a team to discuss practice and its development. At the beginning of the research they did not have an established time to meet on a regular basis; they now have. The research activities also led to careful analysis of best practice in planning in partnership with teachers, and this is explored in the next chapter.

The example below shows the approach an individual assistant took to her analysis of a week's work and the planning for it. There are more examples in Appendix 8 and on the website, and the variety of their work is also evident in the examples. Sharing these sets of evidence led to much discussion and development.

HARROW VI TEAM

FLOW CHART SHOWING PLANNING PROCEDURE

Advantages		**What Can Go Wrong**
Week to plan adaptations. Pre-teach if nec. Look for other resources.	Weekly meeting with teacher. Discuss lesson context for next week	Teacher not available Teacher has not planned. Lesson content changed due to unforeseen circumstances.
Reasonable time to obtain work for adaptation	Obtain work sheets/textbooks for use next week	Worksheets/textbooks not available.
Sufficient time to braille/ refocus etc. Able to consider layout.	Braille worksheets/tactile diagrams/other resources.	Last minute brailling not always possible (location/ noise/need to support in lesson/complicated layout).
Sufficient time to speak to child and prepare him/her for lesson.	Prepare child as required. Go through worksheets if if necessary. Specialist teacher to pre-teach if necessary.	Insufficient time to prepare child, resulting in degrees of exclusion.
Teacher aware of adaptations/layout. Better able to facilitate independence.	Give printed copy of adapted worksheets etc. to teacher if there are significant differences.	Teacher less able to support effectively. Hinders child's independence.
LSA aware of lesson content leading to more effective support.	Support in lesson if required.	Some lessons not instantly adaptable. LSA unable to prepare if content of lesson requires pre-learning.

Another **LEA service, Salford Behaviour Support** (later the **Primary Partnership Service**), also considered forms of flexibility of deployment. As the acting teacher-in-charge, Yvette said, 'Our service to schools is all about flexibility of response, whilst planning for each individual child's needs through planning, curriculum and review meetings.' However, as staff respond, often on an emergency basis, they have to think on their feet. Making sense of the best forms of response in a range of circumstances was an area that they decided they should consider more closely, particularly if this meant that the skills involved might have implications for training.

In evaluating their responses to flexible strategy development the team highlighted the following issues in their report in respect of the work of assistants in particular:

• Forward planning is essential
• There should be a code of conduct between agencies
• Health and safety issues need to be considered when working with children on different sites
• How much information staff should be given
• LSAs should attend planning meetings

Across the LEA in **Moorside High School**, flexibility of deployment was currently concerned with subject department link work being undertaken by the research team of Marie, Yvonne and Dave. The learning support base had decided that the faculty link meeting, when one representative from each faculty came to the resource base each half term, was a good forum to discuss the changes and developments the base was making. These were in respect of how all staff in the school saw it and the role of the base assistants in the school. The base staff had already developed a new brochure that they hoped each faculty would discuss in their own team meetings so that they could decide on a range of different ways of working with the assistants. A large display on the corridor notice board also made both students and staff aware of the ways in which the support from the base could be provided. They had already used one meeting to show faculty representatives the first draft of both the student and staff questionnaires about the assistants' roles they had devised. They felt this was a productive discussion, helping them to redraft in more student-friendly language and add questions that the subject teachers thought would be good to find out about from other teachers.

There are some notes on the website drawn from the team's work on the base's publicity and the first draft of the students' questionnaire that the faculty link meeting discussed and revised. Examples of the students' responses can also be found on the website.

In **Harrow**, at **Whitmore High School** the research team of Sneha, Anne, Karen and Angie were pursuing their action plan in relation to flexibility of deployment. The school had already decided to develop faculty attachments, but had not been sure about the most effective way of doing this. The research team felt that the two assistants, Anne and Sneha, who already concentrated their time in geography and maths respectively, should more formally be seen as being attached to these two departments. They already had excellent working relations with staff in those departments and wanted to initiate a carefully planned and evaluated pilot project using the indicators and review questions to guide them. The team felt that they would be able to then learn lessons about the right strategies and planning formats to use, which might be used to inform practice developments with other faculty attachments in the next school year.

This pilot research was carefully planned and comprehensively documented by both the two assistants and the faculty staff. It wasn't without some teething troubles, such as coordinating non-contact time and starting the project in the middle of the academic year when timetables were set, but in the main it was found to be a positive experience. The students seemed to like meeting an assistant who belonged in maths or geography rather than one who followed them through several subjects. The assistants felt they developed advanced subject knowledge and were able to make the curriculum more accessible to students because of this. The teachers were very positive about the work, saying it had really helped them to have someone to plan with in a much less piecemeal way than previously. One issue that was not so positive was the issue of supply teachers and how they worked with assistants, relying heavily on them to provide continuity.

There are reflective comments from the evaluation reports of Sneha and Anne below, illustrating this flexible deployment to curriculum areas. Further notes, including the minutes of a geography departmental meeting showing how Anne was able to be prepared for a whole series of events, appear on the website.

Ryles Park High School in Cheshire was also exploring the flexible deployment of its assistants. The team as a whole, in their professional development reviews, had all said which faculties they were interested in, confident about and liked working in. Nominally then before they began the research, they all had one faculty to which they were attached, but some, because of their skills or for organisational reasons, were also linked to another. The research team, Carolyn, Sam and Rosemary, wanted to evaluate this more closely using the indicators and review questions. It would help them in making explicit on their job descriptions, and at professional development review time, the specific accountabilities under the 'curriculum' dimension that each assistant undertook. This would make clear how their specific curriculum knowledge and skills were being deployed in the school. It was also helpful in respect of making clear to the LEA that the students with statements were indeed receiving effective curriculum access and support despite the fact that it was not from the 'nominally' allocated person whose contract was 'tied to' an individual student.

This extract from Carolyn's job description makes reference to her particular contributions in maths.

> Key accountabilities: to continue as the link liaison person with the mathematics department by attending all relevant meetings, held both in and out of school. This role also includes involvement in the mathematics pilot scheme. I wish the following contributions to the school community

to be recognised: Designing and producing colour coordinated, laminated magnetic 'KeyWords' for mathematics department. The set-up and organisation of SuccessMaker for the literacy/mathematics Summer Schools at Ryles Park.

WHITMORE HIGH

INDICATORS OF EFFECTIVE PRACTICE WITH LEARNING SUPPORT ASSISTANTS

One of the curriculum areas we had decided to work with was the Maths department. Having worked with Clive Davis (Maths teacher) for the second curriculum year, I feel helped extremely. I knew how he worked and was aware of my roles and responsibilities in the classroom.

I can not emphasise how much an introduction to the class can make such a difference. The first time I supported Clive in a Maths lesson, he introduced me and said 'you are very fortunate to have two adults in this lesson, Miss Radia and myself'. He carried on saying 'Miss Radia is here to help you as much as I am...'. Although this introduction was two years ago I feel like it was yesterday. This made me think the teacher was happy to have support and appreciated it.

Since the start of the project, Clive, Helen (Maths teacher), Angie (governor), Anne (Learning Assistant) and myself had an initial meeting. After this Clive, Anne and myself have had meetings on an ad hoc basis (the reasons for this are in the 'difficulties' section).

The general direction of the lessons were discussed. We also decided to focus on specific students. We tried to make one particular student more independent and another two students more focused on their work.

Outcomes
- The relationship between Clive, Anne and myself improved further.
- The particular student whose independence we tried to increase, achieved this. However, the two students who we tried to make more work focused remained the same.
- By simple 'thank you for your support' comments from the teacher made us feel appreciated .
- All students accepted support.

Sneha

Progress Report: 1.03.01

Becoming part of a specific department
I am enjoying working in the Geography department and feel there are many benefits in being attached to one area of school.

I am beginning to build up a good working relationship with the three teachers in the department and I do feel they benefit from having a regular T.A. on their team.

I feel I am definitely becoming more focused with the subject of Geography and am beginning to remember to ask teachers for information about the next lesson, time permitting. When you are going into many different subject areas I feel it is much more casual and there is not as much opportunity to speak with the teachers.

Anne

In discussion the assistants are enthusiastic about developing departmental links. They feel that they are able to play to their strengths and interests, and to support teachers and students more effectively, and they like the fact that other members of the team cover subjects they feel less confident in.

In addition the team also devised a policy statement documenting their practice of deploying assistants flexibly which was circulated to the management team. The deputy head, John, facilitated this, and it went through some revisions before being published more widely in the school. The aim was to make all new staff aware, and to remind existing staff and governors and parents that this was the practice that now existed in the school. Its status remains draft at this stage. There have been positive comments from Ofsted inspectors about the way in which the school was playing to the assistants' strengths, in respect of support for the curriculum. Specifically, the Ofsted inspectors made the following comment:

> The work of the school's teaching assistants is good. They are well qualified, know the pupils well and provide effective support in the classroom.

In **Park Lane School**, also in **Cheshire**, there had been developments in flexibility of deployment through the ongoing work. Senior management and the research team were making sure that assistants were taking a full part in leading staff meetings for policy development and for staff development purposes. This was felt to be an important way to use their strengths and talents, and particular knowledge about certain issues. As the head teacher Dave, said in a note,

> I have much evidence of team and whole school staff meetings where classroom assistants take a full and sometimes leading part in school development issues, e.g. most recently (15th March, 2001), reviewing our policy and approach to children with Asthma and the Healthy School Initiative.

The attention to the roles and specific responsibilities of assistants in **Parkes Field School in Salford** also resulted in some forms of flexibility that was noted by outsiders to the school. Ofsted inspectors were impressed with what they described as 'seamless teamwork'. Some of this had stemmed from the work that the research team had done on redefining roles and responsibilities. They had, in the eyes of the inspectors, been working so flexibly, creatively and effectively in their class and departmental teams that this was noted and commended. Of course the research team and whole school team were very pleased, and Anthea, the head, said to the inspectors that these developments were in good part the direct result of the work they had done within their research action plan. There were additional verbal comments from the inspectors about the effective use that was made of the assistants' skills.

These examples are mostly, of course, closely linked to the ways in which the schools and services were carefully defining or redefining the roles and responsibilities of TAs. The processes in some schools or services, such as Ryles

Park and Vaughan First and Middle, began through already having developed the flexibility that they had built into their practice. There was the recognition of the need to represent this in the rewritten job descriptions, drawing the assistants into the task, using their actual experiences. Others, such as Grange First, had started with a need to establish job descriptions that reflected an intended development of flexibility in the role, particularly as they set about increasing flexible forms of support for the curriculum. In whichever way these activities were undertaken by the lead researchers in the schools and the services, they took practice and policy-writing forward in each setting.

The next chapter explores some details about the ways in which the researchers used the indicators connected with teacher and assistant partnerships to develop more precise understandings of how to develop effective strategies that had an impact on classroom practice. Many of these activities were directly linked into their intentions to develop flexibility of deployment, often in the need to recognise the skills and competencies of the assistants that could enhance teaching and learning for all children.

9 Planning for teamwork with teachers

The teams of researchers in the schools and services developed some interesting and effective strategies for encouraging partnership and learning between teachers and assistants. In many cases they had not specifically focused on this area from the beginning, but they had been led into it from other points in their initiatives. The examples described in this chapter are linked to the discussion of more conceptual issues presented in Chapter 4.

In **Harrow, the VI Service team**, Janice, Rosie, Jaquie, Kathryn, Margaret and Elizabeth, were led to think carefully about planning with teachers and developing their partnerships as they worked to support children with visual impairment. As was explained in the previous chapter their analysis of their working week and the liaison they undertook with teachers caused them to think about the planning processes. They drafted a set of procedures for planning with teachers, one for primary and one for secondary. The emphasis of these procedures was on enabling primary teachers to take responsibility for the whole class and for secondary students to receive their curriculum access materials from the subject teachers at the same time as their peers. These outcomes are expected in the absence of the assistant rather than necessarily in her presence. If the assistants are present they are likely to be carrying out an observation role in order to feed into planning and feedback processes and discussions with the teacher.

During the course of the research the team manager, Elizabeth, was seconded from Harrow to the Royal National Institute for the Blind (RNIB) as its London-based senior education officer for London and the South-East. Within her new role she was able to use the lessons learnt during the research with her team in Harrow to inform the writing, advice and guidance that she was now undertaking. This included an article for *Visability*, the RNIB magazine, of spring 2001. In it she explained about the action research project work that the assistants and she had been involved in, the indicators they chose to focus on; a set of outcomes resulting from good planning; and she included the two sets of planning procedures, for primary and secondary contexts. The intention was that other VI support teams and their assistants and leaders would be able to use them as guidance for their work. She was also devising training programmes for wider dissemination using what had been learnt during the research project in Harrow. These are detailed in Chapter 12.

The extracts from the *Visability* magazine article below illustrate the value of teachers and assistants planning effectively together. The whole article appears on the website.

Approach to planning and adaptation in a primary school

Identify a time/frequency for planning
Identify who should be there

Class teacher **brings written plans** to meeting, which will include:

- Lesson aims
- Content of lessons
- Learning objectives
- Pages of books to be used
- Worksheets to be used

Teacher/LSA/Specialist Teacher (VI) go through plans in order to identify:

- Teaching approaches to be used
- Need for any pre-teaching
- Teaching points of more complex materials
- Need for any in-class support
- Opportunities for small group work

Specialist teacher (VI) and LSA meet to analyse the best way to adapt materials depending on information received at previous meeting with the class teacher

LSA adapts materials ➤ print copy given to teacher

Materials given to pupil by teacher at the same time as peers

Teacher takes responsibility for the learning of the whole class.

Approach to planning and adaptation in a secondary school

LSA obtains **schemes of work** from subject teachers

These will include:
- Topics to be covered
- Details of each lesson
- Lesson aims (general)
- Expected outcomes
- Page numbers (of books to be used)
- Copies of worksheets (numbered)
- Homework

LSA goes through them/looks at materials

Will go back to **subject teacher** to get more specific information/clarification on content or teaching approach to be used (if necessary)

Will go to **specialist teacher** (visual impairment) to sort out issues relating to braille/tactile production/ approaches to adaptation

Produces materials

Passes the materials through system (existing or set up to suit individual requirements) to subject teachers

Student receives materials from **subject teacher** at the same time as peers.

Detailed planning with teachers on the curriculum was undertaken and documented as part of the research by two of the assistants in the team, Kathryn and Janice. There are examples in both Appendix 9 and on the website of the planning done for geography with the teachers and by Kathryn herself before lessons. Janice has also provided a reflective account of the process.

Part of the team's research plan was to draw pupils into the evaluative processes to see if they had noticed an impact on the effectiveness of their curriculum access and support as a result of these planning processes. This proved more difficult than was at first thought, for a variety of reasons. A group interview was attempted with children who are blind and of different ages, but the group dynamics were not very good and the data gathered was not as illuminating as the team had hoped. However, undaunted, they intend to try again as they feel that they should listen to what the pupils have to say.

At **Whitmore High School in Harrow** Anne and Sneha had been developing the faculty attachment work with teachers, including Seri, head of geography, and Clive, in the maths department. Their starting point was in the area of flexibility of deployment but this had led to some detailed scrutiny of partnership work. Anne has kept a detailed diary of her work attached to the geography department, which includes her initial thoughts, the activities she carried out, her planning with Seri, the geography department meetings she attended, Seri's evaluations and her own thoughts as the work developed and she reflected on its impact. This record has been shared and discussed with the learning support team as part of the ongoing research and as they plan further faculty attachment in the new academic year of 2001. A key element that is described is the planning and teamwork between the teacher and the assistant about particular lessons and activities and the evaluation of this.

One of the interesting messages they took from the evaluation was the experience of working with supply or cover teachers and the additional pressures this can put on assistants. Since it arose so clearly this issue has been brought up at management board and governing body meetings.

There are comments on the website from both Anne as assistant and Angie as governor, about teamwork between teachers and assistants. Angie, in working on project coordination, saw positive outcomes for students, teachers and assistants.

In **Harrow**, at **Grange First School** Lynne and the assistants were also working on how to draw the assistants into the teachers' planning and teamwork as this had been an area identified in their questionnaire enquiry analysis. They and the headteacher, Sue, felt that developing partnership in curriculum approaches would lead to more flexibility of deployment and clarification of the developing role within the classroom. It was hoped that from using joint staff development opportunities the more effective forms of planning would follow. There is more detail in Chapter 12 about some of the staff development meeting agendas, focusing on the literacy strategy, behaviour management and in the future IT.

One of the first staff meetings addressed a set of questions about planning, in the context of the revised assistant job descriptions and newly formulated flexible working arrangements. The meeting also heard from the assistants about how one teacher and TA had developed an effective partnership in preparation for working in year teams. The record of a staff development meeting on the ways for teachers to plan and work effectively with assistants and questions to address, appears below.

GRANGE FIRST SCHOOL – INSET
MONDAY 22 JANUARY 2001
Working with Teaching Assistants – effective teaching and learning

OBJECTIVES

1. To familiarise teachers with the revised Teaching Assistant job description.
2. To identify current good practice.
3. To consider practical implications of the revised job description for effective teacher/Teaching Assistant partnerships.
4. To agree effective practice to support Teaching Assistants.

AGENDA

3.45–4.00 Introduction (Lynne) and read through Teaching Assistant's job description.

4.00–4.05 Identifying current good practice (brief look at Catherine and Varsha's partnership)

4.05–4.35 Work in Year Teams to discuss and complete questionnaire relating to good practice.

4.35–5.00 Feedback from year teams about questionnaire. (Lynne to scribe responses on flipchart in order to establish agreement on effective practice.)

A future session will look at developing classroom practice and teaching and learning strategies. Long-term aim is to establish a whole school policy and set of guidelines to enhance teaching and learning through effective teacher/TA partnerships.

QUESTIONNAIRE – WORKING WITH TEACHING ASSISTANTS

1. How can Teaching Assistants be included in planning?

2. How can plans be communicated to Teaching Assistants?

3. What do Teaching Assistants need to know about the children with special needs they are supporting?

4. How could the Teaching Assistants contribute to record-keeping?

5. In what ways can the teacher develop the Teaching Assistants' skills?

6. In what ways can the school develop the Teaching Assistants' skills?

7. What training should school provide to support teachers with Teaching Assistants?

Upton Priory Junior School in Cheshire addressed ways of improving teacher–assistant partnerships in relation to setting up mechanisms for liaison between two different sets of meetings. These were the teachers' business staff meetings and the assistants' meetings. Ann and Karen and the team established a system where one of the team made a record for the teachers of any relevant points coming from their meetings that teachers should know about or act upon. This then went on the agenda of the teachers' next meeting and was elaborated where necessary by an assistant who attended the meeting. Likewise items for the assistants were recorded and passed on to them. Of course, this does not mean verbal information was not being passed frequently and outside formal meeting situations as well, but this was introduced so that courses of action and responsibility were clearly recorded and accountable. This was an insurance that teachers and assistants were all well-informed and the teamwork between them would be enhanced. There were also staff development meetings that everyone attended, teachers and assistants together, on literacy, for example, where this system of recording was unnecessary. However, the point was also being reinforced that the assistants had good reasons for needing regular team meetings as well as teachers.

There are examples on the website reproduced from the 'minutes notebooks' that were kept showing how information was exchanged between the two meeting forums. In the teachers' minutes there is a reference to assistants having literacy training, and essential information at a practical level (they would be off-timetable) and at a skills level (the teachers would be aware of their new skills). In the assistants' minutes the list of playground duties and representatives' attendance at the teachers' meeting was to be added to the agenda for the teachers' meeting.

When **Ryles Park High School in Cheshire** was inspected it was noted in the Ofsted report how effective the teamwork between teachers and assistants was and how this led to positive experiences for all children as well as those with significant special needs. In developing this effective teamwork they have thus been able to become a more inclusive school.

The inspectors said:

> Teachers make effective use of learning support assistants' skills and fully involve them in lesson planning. Teachers and their assistants take a genuine interest in each pupil, providing good advice and recognising pupils' efforts and successes. The school has a sufficient number of suitably qualified teachers who work closely with a good team of teaching assistants so that pupils' individual needs are regularly supported within mainstream lessons.

The team had devised and circulated the following document on assistant/teacher partnership amongst all staff so that they had clear guidance and this had helped to develop these effective partnerships. This is the kind of document that NQTs, for example, and newly appointed teachers in any school would find helpful and could use when planning with assistants. In fact, given that many experienced teachers have had no formal training in how to work with assistants, they too are likely to find it helpful.

RYLES PARK

LSA/Teacher Partnership

Most effective as a **Team**:

> same **message**
> same **strategies**
> same **goals**

First AGREE:

> class **rules**
> class **routines** e.g. entry to room
> marking work
> equipment loan
> **discipline roles**

The LSA needs to know:

> what will **happen** in the lesson
> how can they **support** this
> what **differentiation** can they offer
> what **expertise** can they offer.

good communication!! ➡ **ESSENTIAL**

From the beginning:

> what are the shared **goals**
> **who** does **what**
> **discipline** – methods, roles,
> **teaching methods** and **roles** e.g. role during
> class teaching
> question time
> group work
> written tasks
> reading
> about the group e.g. their character, ability, strengths,
> individual needs etc.
> * **remember the LSA** may have a lot to offer here.
> who do the children think the LSA is? – **explain** their role.

When a new topic starts the LSA needs to:

> look at **material**
> understand teaching **methodology**
> understand **goals**
> know what help groups or individuals may need.

Other Issues

Feedback – This can, if you're brave enough, be incredibly valuable – simply ask the LSA what they think of how the lesson went.

Department meetings – Invite an LSA – they will feel more able to contribute.

These examples showing how the indicators and review questions in the Good Practice Guide can stimulate the development of assistant/teacher partnerships are not extensive, as the schools mainly focused on other issues in their action research plans. The quality of these examples, however, leads to positive messages about the place of planning in this work and the need for senior staff to recognise its importance and facilitate time for this in the timetabling of the school or service.

However, it is worth thinking about how a school or service would respond to the following review questions and the kinds of strategies to be used in that setting either to generate data or to move practice forward. Perhaps some of the ideas in Chapter 6 will have provided ideas about the processes best suited to a particular school or service. These questions focus on teachers and assistants working cooperatively together. They are a selection from one of the GPG indicators about cooperative working between teachers and TAs:

Creating partnerships with teachers

Indicator 3:1 TAs work co-operatively with teachers to support the learning and participation of pupils

- Do TAs understand the purpose of lesson activities?
- Are TAs involved in the planning of specific lessons where teachers and TAs share the classroom?
- Are TAs involved in flexible decision-making about plans during lessons?
- Do TAs and teachers plan in ways that demonstrate to pupils their commitment to teamwork?

In Appendix 4 some examples of activities based on the ideas in the Good Practice Guide and in this research are provided; some of these focus directly on teachers and assistants learning to work more effectively together. They are edited versions of longer sets of questions and are the ones like those we used at the introductory workshops to help the participants establish an overview and understanding of the Guide's contents.

10 Drawing parents, governors and others into the work of assistants

This chapter considers the ways in which assistants are able to develop effective working relationships, liaison and communication with other people (other than with class teachers, which was explored in the last chapter) who are directly concerned in the process of education. The issues outlined in Chapter 4 underpin at a conceptual level what is written here.

The people who work with TAs, referred to in this chapter, range from the learning support coordinator and supply teachers, to advisory staff who visit the school from the LEA, including senior officers. They include parents, governors, related professionals such as therapists and medical or social service personnel, and educational psychologists. The contact between them and the TAs should of course be coordinated by a manager/teacher as part of a strategic plan, so that lines of communication and responsibility are clear. The links that TAs can establish with these people are, of course, in addition to their partnerships with the relevant classroom teachers.

In five of the research schools (**Ryles Park High, Puss Bank Infants, Upton Priory Junior, Vaughan First and Middle** and **Grange First**) an outcome of the whole project was the development of closer relations and working practices between learning support coordinators and assistants. They were the 'senior staff' designated by the schools to work with the nominated assistants to carry out the work as 'lead researchers'. The very existence of the project and the action research processes had a significant impact on the existing working relationships between the assistants and their learning support coordinators. Although each small team would have said that they had good working relationships before they joined the research work on the indicators, the first workshop discussions they had about the indicators and review questions made them think carefully about their own teamwork. This led them to rethink their understanding of the role of the assistants in developing and maintaining effective teamwork.

The learning support coordinators in these settings, Rosemary, Catherine, Ann, Sue and Lynne, all saw how important their advocacy on behalf of the assistants was. They used their position and professional status to demonstrate the role they could play in helping to make things happen, although it must be said that they were working with some assistants who were quite capable of making things happen themselves!

Collaborative action research should mean that all participants take responsibility, and assistants have undoubtedly done that. Other senior members of staff, such as the deputy headteachers Lynn in **Parkes Field** or Dave in **Moorside**, also fulfilled the coordination, advocacy and supportive role to their teams. This evidence underlines the need for the presence of managers, in any school undertaking development work, to empower assistants to become 'movers and shakers', but also to be that constant presence at a senior level.

Parents were drawn into the research work in **Moorside High School in Salford** where their perceptions of the role were investigated. This was done through the questionnaire that was drawn up by the lead researchers in consultation with the whole team at the learning support base and also through the faculty link meeting agenda. The review questions were based on those in the indicators of effective practice, but contextualised for Moorside and also in parent-friendly language.

The questions sought to find out how much parents knew about what assistants did and also what they thought about this currently and their ideas for the future. The sample included parents who did not have a child on the register of special needs as well as some who did. The research team was mindful of the fact that all parents should develop a better idea of what assistants did, as any student might, at some time, be supported by an assistant as well as by a teacher. This work with parents has been the most recent part of the Moorside team's research and they are currently analysing the results of their inquiry, in order to take any necessary actions. Examples of responses to the parents' questionnaire can be found on the website.

Whitmore High School's work in involving governors has happened in large part because the lead research team includes Angie, the parent governor in the school with responsibility for special needs. Their decision to ask her to join them at the outset shows how important the school managers already feel their work in partnership with governors is. The presence of Angie throughout the action research has led to a number of positive outcomes. Her understanding of the need for TAs to develop more focused and skilled curriculum knowledge stemmed in part from her own son's experience in the school, but also from the conversations she had had on a regular basis with the assistants themselves in her role as special needs governor.

Because of her strategic presence in terms of influencing the governing body and senior management she was able to support the proposal for the presence of the assistants on the management board. She also made sure that the action research project itself was an agenda item at governors' meetings, thus keeping the valued work of the assistants in the minds of her fellow governors.

There are extracts below from a governors' report to parents, and Angie's own evaluative comments as governor. The information for parents helped in the efforts to raise the profile of assistants with them. The governor's overview in her evaluative comments provides insights into the schoolwide impact of the project that in part occurred as a result of her involvement.

WHITMORE HIGH

*Parent Partnership [from Governors' Report]

Our Governor for Special Educational Needs is Angie Lawrence. We have valued the support she has given us this year. Angie and two of our Learning Assistants, Anne Perring and Sneha Radia, are currently working on a research project with Manchester University. They are looking at the Effective Practice of Learning Assistants in High Schools.

We value our partnership with parents and know that we share the goal of students achieving their best. We welcome feedback and communication from parents, our aim is to have a continuous dialogue with parents. Angie Lawrence can be contacted via the school and welcomes feedback from other parents.

WHITMORE HIGH

Angie Lawrence   March 2001

Outcomes:
- raising the profile of LSAs at management and governors' meetings, thus in turn making all staff aware and think about the role of the LSAs
- fighting for raised profile and suitable pay structure at Governors' Forum level and with the LEA
- plans brought to management board
- inclusion in headteacher's report
- inclusion in annual governors' report to parents
- after discussion and meeting with Maggie, became aware of a need for a place for an LSA on the Management board and on the Governing body, took these ideas to the head and now places are being considered
- raised confidence and self esteem of LSAs involved have been asked to attend INSET
- for longstanding TAs they felt they needed to have an induction guide or guide for TAs, a new handbook had been written and updated by TAs
- meeting in Manchester with other participants of the project. Showed the diversity and disparity of different Boroughs around the country. (pay, job descriptions, values, etc.)
- at interviews and governing body meetings it is possible to raise and maintain awareness of the good practices and ask the right questions.

Being in the position of governor I am able to liaise between teaching staff and TAs, and the head and governors. Being on many committees I am also able to raise awareness of issues of TAs and disseminate information about the good and bad practices that happen in school, Borough and further afield, and especially about the work of the project. I arrange meetings or talk time with the SENCo, Deputy SENCo, Head, Chair of Governors, teachers and TAs to discuss some of the matters that have arisen from the project. At interviews and governing body meetings it is possible to raise and maintain awareness of the good practices started before and developed further with the participation of the Manchester Project.

Salford Primary Partnership Centre and their work with related professionals from health and social services had developed during the course of the action research project. They, Yvette, Sarah and Linda, identified, through the indicator reviews at the first workshop and in discussion at a team meeting, that this was an area for attention. They had felt that the service they provided for certain individuals could be improved with better contacts.

As a result of these closer contacts and better working relationships with the paediatric department at the local hospital they had established more regular liaison with the TAs being fully involved in this. There has also been closer liaison with social services over some vulnerable pupils. Joint meetings in setting up placements of children had also included the assistants and other professionals. In more than one instance, a child had had a more successful experience at a new school because of this.

The extract below from Pupil B's report illustrates this:

> A young boy moved into a new home when his adoption failed, leading to a new school placement. The social worker contacted the school and a planning meeting with the involved parties, including the LSA, was arranged. The following was then put in place: LSA allocation of 16 hours per week; a visit by B to the school to meet class teachers and LSA together; the LSA visited his home and worked with him twice before he started school; B started school on second day after half term when other children had settled after the holiday; the LSA supported the pupil in the classroom, during breaks and lunch period to encourage the formation of appropriate social groups. Support has now decreased to eight hours and he is now spending most of the unstructured part of the school day unsupported.

Parkes Field School had an Ofsted inspection during the time of the research work and the inspectors wrote in their report about aspects of effective practice concerning teamwork in the school. In most of their comments the work of assistants was implicated. There was a note of effective teamwork between assistants, teachers and other professionals visiting the school. The inspectors spoke of the teamwork where the ethos of the school is enforced, resulting in effective support for pupils.

There was also a written comment about 'seamless teamwork' in relation to assistants' partnerships with other agencies and especially parents. In addition, also to their credit, there were comments about the ways in which supply teachers and assistants worked together effectively, with assistants providing continuity where these teachers were not so familiar with the contextual routines and the children.

The following are extracts from the Ofsted report:

- Teaching and support staff enforce effectively the ethos of the school with the help they give to the pupils.
- The school has created a seamless partnership with parents which effectively harnesses the efforts of teachers, support staff, therapists and parents to ensure pupils' physical and personal development.
- The teachers, teaching assistants and therapists work as a very close team.

- In one class which was taught by a supply teacher during the week of the inspection, there was the good use of data collection…in this lesson the contribution that the assistants made to the smooth running and organisation was commendable, as the supply teacher was new to the school.

The Parkes Field research team also wrote a briefing paper in preparation for the combining of three schools to make the new school. This briefing paper (below) was for all other professionals who would be working in the new school team, outlining the purposes and outcomes of the work to date, and was circulated amongst all members of staff in the new school.

PARKES FIELD

'Indicators of Effective Practice with Learning Support Assistants'
Joint Manchester University and LEA pilot research

A brief outline of the project to inform colleagues

During the year 2000, staff at Parkes Field took part in an action research project, looking into effective practice with teaching assistants. The research was part of a follow-up pilot project, using indicators produced during the original DfEE commissioned project carried out by Manchester University. A group of four staff attended the meetings and workshops, liaising with colleagues from Salford, Harrow and Cheshire. Dr Maggie Balshaw and Dr Peter Farrell from the University of Manchester led the project. Each of the schools involved used the indicators provided by the university to analyse and evaluate their own practice. Below is a brief summary of the project:

Feb 00 **Invited by LEA to take part in project**
Mar 00 **First meeting held with Salford school participants to draw up research plans**
May 00 **Visit to school by Manchester University researchers to discuss work-in-progress**
Jun 00 **Joint evaluation workshop with three LEAs and presentations from each group**
Nov 00 **Meeting of Salford schools to review progress and discuss the evaluation report**
Response to the Good Practice Guide
Discussion about publications, including a proposed book

The outcomes of the research carried out at Parkes Field school were as follows:

- Revised job descriptions
- Half-termly TA meetings
- Portfolios of achievement (voluntary)
- Cameos written by some staff

This is a very brief summary of the project. More detailed information is available and copies will be left in school. Now that the main part of the research is complete, Maggie and Peter have decided to write a book based on their findings. They have invited all the schools involved to play a part in the production of the book. If anyone is interested in the project and would like to get involved please contact Lynn Monks or Angela Macdonald at Parkes Field for details.

One particular contribution to wider school activities was not directly related to this action research. However, it is mentioned here to illustrate the potential for involving TAs in this way. At **Upton Priory Junior School** TAs collaborated with parents in fundraising for a charity for disabled children. Karen developed a quiz about food that motivated entries from many people, including research colleagues in the project. The TAs also sought sponsors for a parachute jump by TAs Karen and Kath. Is there no end to these assistants' talents!

Staff at **Ryles Park High School**, when devising the assistants' new job descriptions, were careful to include sections about wider contributions that take account of the range of the assistants' individual skills. This went beyond support for the curriculum in departmental attachment work to, for example, their contributions to lunchtime clubs; liaison with parents; involvement in the action research project; additional meetings such as those attended by parents for their learning about their children's curriculum and so on. These contributions were then taken into consideration at professional development review interviews. This meant they were not seen as 'add-ons', but as part of the working day. They also reflect the particular interests and talents of Sam, Linda and Carolyn and all the other assistants in the team.

The following examples from the job descriptions illustrate this point:

Sam: Lunchtime – motor co-ordination Club, 5 sessions per week (every day); Support Dance 2000 workshop; 'Support Staff' governor.

Linda: Producing 'Key Words' for the Drama department; Attend Samba workshops.

Carolyn: Involvement with Manchester University/DfEE Research Project regarding the role of Teaching Assistants; Attend 'Open evenings' to explain the role of SuccessMaker within Ryles Park School; Facilitate evening opportunities for parents to experience 'SuccessMaker' with their children.

In considering 'outsiders' to the school or service it would be remiss to omit the need to work in collaboration with LEA officers, keeping them informed of developments in practice and in principle, and their role in supporting these endeavours. Senior officers in each of the LEAs were involved from the beginning of the action research, helping to identify schools to become involved in attending the LEA workshops and the evaluation conference at Manchester University. Elaine Gardner of Harrow, Fintan Bradley and Dave Richards of Cheshire and Judith Jones of Salford were all in some way involved in developing LEA practice in support of the project schools.

Amongst the outcomes from this was a closer scrutiny in one LEA of the wording on assistants' contracts, taking account of their relationship to statements for individuals, and a more flexible view of their role in the local area where the group of schools was situated. Assistants were assured of continuity in their role in September 2000 that had previously been more tenuous, because of the nature of their contracts. A training and qualifications review was carried out that was directly connected to one LEA's role in provision for assistants, in part stimulated by discussions held during the action research project.

This chapter has explored the nature of the need to make sure that all people connected with a school or service are as far as possible informed about and, where appropriate, involved in the work of assistants. This has the potential to lead to much more effective practices in the way assistants are valued and deployed so that their roles are understood. The next chapter goes on to consider how these practices can be developed through the establishment of team meetings and support for assistants, from managers and from within the assistant group itself.

11 Creating opportunities for team development

This chapter deals with the development of teams of assistants in the schools and services involved in the action research. Team development was explored in Chapter 5 in relation to the outcomes of the original research and this chapter links those findings to the action research outcomes.

Assistants' actual involvement in the action research project itself led to different perspectives on the purposes and, indeed, the necessity for team development in many of the schools. Their collaborative action research necessitated drawing up an action plan that had a series of meetings of groups of people or the 'lead researchers' on a regular basis. For some groups this was done in their existing meetings, for others a series of extra meetings happened. This process was facilitated by the senior colleagues with support from the school and service leaders.

The reasons for having meetings as a regular part of school practice were made clear in Chapter 5. The schools and services involved in the action research in the main had already begun to hold regular meetings of the assistants' team within their working hours, in school time. They had moved away from the assumption that it was acceptable to ask assistants to stay on in their own time in order to do this, and considered that they should be meeting in paid time. They also saw that the teaching staff understood the need for this, accepting their release from the classroom if need be.

One such school is **Vaughan First and Middle, Harrow**. The team already met on a fortnightly basis on a day of the week when most of the assistants were in school. There were, because of part-time contracts, two or three assistants who were not timetabled to be there but who came into or back to school for the meeting. When the lead researchers, Surinder and Jackie the assistants, and Sue, the deputy head and learning support coordinator, used the indicators to review practice in the school, they identified induction and job descriptions to be two areas on which to focus. They realised that they would be able to raise these at the next scheduled existing meeting of the team. Later, an occasional additional meeting was added, where necessary, but in the main their meetings were already there to facilitate the process.

However, their enquiries caused them to redefine some of the processes involved and also the purposes for their meetings. These ranged from how they kept records; who was responsible for the agenda; who called and led the meeting; when they met as a team, chaired/led by one of their number; how decisions were followed through and communicated to other staff. They used meeting time to brainstorm their ideas about the contents of job descriptions, and what was needed for a booklet to support the induction procedures for new assistants. They used their own previous experiences to inform these processes. They developed stronger problem-solving skills individually and as a team. There was also a review of the way in which members of the team might be asked to lead at in-service training opportunities. These matters of induction and staff development are dealt with in more detail in the next chapter.

The agenda for team meetings is pinned on the staff room notice board, and the first items are suggested by Sue as chair; the assistants add ideas they want on the agenda. The minutes are kept and circulated with clear action points for the team and others, including school management, to take. The handwritten example on the website is the actual agenda for 7 February 2001. The record of that meeting follows. There is close correlation between the two, and clearly the different handwriting shows that several people contributed to the list in a democratic process. There are also some comments about the importance of the meeting agendas from an assistant herself.

Again in **Harrow, Grange First School** also began to keep a more careful record of their meetings. Their review using the indicators, carried out firstly by Brenda and Lynne, led them to consider the ways in which the need for meeting time was met. They also thought about how they should use this meeting time, i.e. how the agenda was put together and by whom, and how it could be recorded and acted upon. From this came an agenda jointly decided for each meeting. A record was kept of each one, and this typically would include: an information update; an action research project update; an update on special needs reviews and practices; items about current training amongst the group – who was doing what and dissemination to the group where appropriate; and business items such as AOB, and the next meeting date. There is a meeting agenda, and the handwritten record of that meeting on the website.

Clearly, this activity made the meetings much more formal and carefully planned. The outcomes were positive, with assistants feeling that there was real structure and purpose to their meetings. They knew that the rest of the school team should also be aware of the professional manner in which the senior management was treating them. This set an ethos of value and also reflective practice within the school as a whole. The assistant team was, in a sense, taking a lead on how to develop practice through action research, with the lead and support of Lynne.

In **Upton Priory Junior School, Cheshire** the research team of Karen, Katherine and Ann was busily establishing the principle of having meetings during the working week, drawing the whole assistant team into this. The team itself constructed the meeting agenda and a careful record was kept of the meeting. Problem-solving was high on the agenda very often. In one such set of minutes there is a record of the fact that a letter had been sent to Cheshire LEA personnel department about their concerns over 'single status' pay proposals and the impact they felt it would have on them. Another item recorded the fact that they wished to have attendance from a member of a senior management team at least once a month, so that they 'are aware of what we are discussing and to help iron out any problems that come up'.

Forms of support they gave each other were also explored and expressed during the meetings. Self-esteem was clearly an important purpose for their meetings. There has been a significant recognition of the ways in which at an everyday, often at an impromptu, level they offer each other support of a practical and moral nature. They felt that this was an important part of the positive feel their work has in the school. There are comments on the website on the kinds of support they have experienced from one another as a result of the team-building ethos.

In an early meeting that they held, they reflected on the aspects of their role that they felt were rewarding, challenging and stressful and discussed the causes of these feelings. They attempted to establish links between these feelings and their existing roles and responsibilities and also others' perceptions of their role. This process helped them to really critique where they were at as individuals and as a team. It increased their 'problem-solving' capacity. It was also good for their self-esteem as they recognised there was much to feel reinforced about as well as to develop further, either in their team or through other people in the school. The record of this meeting and the next is below. There is a record of an assistants' business meeting on the website.

The research team at **Moorside High School in Salford** were also considering the purpose and processes of their team meetings. Marie and Yvonne felt that their meetings needed a little more structure as a result of their discussions about the indicators. They changed from meeting at lunchtime on Fridays when there were constant interruptions and it was voluntary. They now meet in period five, week one (the school works a two-week timetable) so that it is seen as working time, is 'protected' and, to a large extent, is uninterrupted. This is described in an item on the website. This revision has meant a much better and more consistent attendance and more productive agendas, with careful records kept of the meeting and action points arising. The learning support coordinator is present but does not lead, the assistants do that themselves. The deputy head, Dave, helped to coordinate at management level the changes involved in timetabling that took all assistants out of class on period five, with the teachers informed about the reasons for this.

The **Visual Impairment Team in Harrow** were also coming to the view that the meetings called to carry out their action research using the indicators were drawing them together more closely as a team. This was proving to be positive for their self-esteem; explaining to the colleagues about how they had each developed their practices and skills was a boost for them, and meant that they were appreciating each other's skills as well as their own in a much deeper way. As a team they then learnt from each other. They also grew more adept at problem-solving as a group. The benefit of meetings of this kind was not lost on them or on their team leader, Elizabeth. They became an established part of team practice, and continued when their new team leader Helen took over. In the next chapter there is some more detail about staff development outcomes from their meetings.

UPTON PRIORY

- We had a good meeting with Maggie Balshaw and all the LSAs. We outlined the project and our particular focus and all agreed that this was a priority which would underpin further discussion and progress. Maggie encouraged us to consider various aspects of our jobs under the headings Rewarding, Challenging and Stressful.

- Rewarding aspects include:
  - A sense of achievement in enabling a child to gain learning/physical independence.
  - Working as a team.
  - Good relationships with child/parents/teacher.
  - Residential visits.
- Challenging aspects include:
  - Working with behavioural problems.
  - Working with a new child, recognising skills/needs and developing these.
  - Organising work with small groups.
  - Motivating and holding a child's interest
  - Developing confidence in particular skills, e.g. swimming.
  - Delivering the Additional Literacy Strategy.
  - Getting teaching staff to take notice of the child.
  - A lack of consistency of approach by the teaching staff.
  - Being included in games and dancing.
  - Residential trips.
- Stressful aspects include:
  - Not always knowing in advance what is happening in the lessons.
  - Frequent changes of instructions at short notice.
  - Not having enough time to do essential regular activities, e.g. physiotherapy.
The main issues to emerge from this discussion:
- Communication.
- Consistency.

- At their next meeting, the LSAs began to discuss the job description. They discussed the various aspects of their role and looked at some examples of job descriptions (see attached) to see how their role might best be outlined. At an INSET day in July, we hope to bring all this thinking together to write the job description, to plan how to discuss the role with teaching staff, particularly the communication and consistency issues and how to address the issue of management structure and support.

Ann Parr and Karen Woodall.

In **Ryles Park High School in Cheshire** the assistants have developed, from their review using the indicators, a pattern of team meetings led sometimes by the assistants themselves, sometimes by or with Rosemary, their learning support coordinator, and with a joint responsibility for the termly programmes and agendas. At the beginning of the action research the team all completed and discussed a short questionnaire specifically designed to elicit the assistants' views of their role, job descriptions and particular training needs in respect of the curriculum. Team meetings were used to then plan what actions should be taken in order to address some of the issues raised. Problem-solving of this kind was a key feature of their meetings.

The questionnaire shown on the website was a data-gathering exercise that led to further developments and actions. These actions were taken in part by the team in their own meetings and in part by others, such as the senior management team.

The examples of meeting agendas and outcomes below and on the website provide insights into what was on the assistants' minds and the actions that were being taken as a result. They also show evidence of follow-up activities from the questionnaire outcomes. One item is a draft of the notes drawn up by Linda in order to lead a staff development session for the team about the key points she wished to make about the DfEE induction training on literacy. She had attended this and was to disseminate to the team in a regular meeting in order that they all benefited. Overall these items illustrate the rich variety of their activities during team meetings.

RYLES PARK HIGH

TA MEETING
12.15pm 20th November 2000
Seminar Room

Present: SH, CA, MA, LS, VB, CN, ML, KS, JD, NP, BM, JH, RAB

Key Points:
- Feedback to the group by TAs who had been on training courses. LS, JD, SH. Wonderful written accounts circulated to be put together in a folder in the staff room to give wider access.
- Update on job descriptions for Manchester University research project. Feedback from other TAs on draft job description document.
- Blank documents distributed to be filled in by all TAs now.
- Brainstorm training needs to be fed back to Dave (?) on 23.11.00.
- Circulated breakdown of working hours for 32.5 hour week for TAs consideration. To be discussed next meeting.

Next meeting to be held on Monday 18th December in the Seminar Room.

A common theme running through the meetings described above is that of staff development in all its forms, and these matters are explored more fully in the next chapter. It is sometimes difficult to separate the aspects of developing confidence, self-esteem and problem-solving skills with learning and staff development. In fact it would be foolish to try too hard as they are so closely linked and interdependent for much of the time. However, the examples in this chapter explored specific aspects that were important, not least the principle of assistants being treated as professionals who meet as a team in paid time.

12 Devising induction strategies, professional development reviews and records of achievement

This chapter focuses on the issues concerning staff development in its widest sense in relation to assistants' needs, entitlements and responsibilities. In the conclusion to the last chapter the links were made between the team development of assistants, leading to increased self-esteem and the capacity to problem-solve, and staff development. Indeed, the team meetings that the schools and services have either refined or established for their assistants are mainly used for the purposes of staff development within the school or service. The issues in the last chapter and this exploring the links between team and staff development were discussed at a conceptual level in Chapter 5.

There are broadly three major areas where staff development can occur for assistants. One is in the classroom with the teachers they work with, where both can learn about practice. Secondly, they learn in school in a wider forum such as their own team meetings or staff development sessions (in department teams or the whole school). Thirdly, they may also learn outside school within LEA or from further/higher education courses. Examples of all three of these were found in the schools carrying out their action research.

Beginning with the very first stages, of learning in the job, the team at **Vaughan First and Middle School in Harrow** was concerned with the indicator and review questions related to induction procedures, and Surinder, Jackie and Sue decided this was an important issue. They had previously done some induction but not in the formalised and informed way they thought was necessary. The assistants in the team recognised that they had 'insider' knowledge of what it felt like to start a new job. Some of this was very recent, and as they knew their team was to expand considerably in the next year they saw it as a crucial target in their action research plan. They used team meetings to brainstorm all the things that from their own experience they knew it was essential to know about or where to find out about, on the first day, in the first week, in the first term, and so on. This gave them a comprehensive set of ideas that they then sorted out and organised into what was needed when and where it should be found.

The outcome was a booklet for new staff written by the team from their own experience. Their new colleagues received it very appreciatively at the start of the next term. The first page appears on the website and includes essential information about the workings of the school. This had been seen as essential from the experiences of assistants joining the team previously.

However, the written information was not the only strategy they considered. Mentoring or 'buddying' also was an aspect that they felt to be important. This personal touch was one they would have liked themselves, as they looked back at their own beginnings in the school. They set up a system for the new school year where all assistants who were experienced mentored a newly appointed assistant into the school way of life. This was also warmly received. However, another outcome from this was the staff development that also occurred for those who took on the buddying role. They learnt from the experience some new skills which they found to be rewarding and which improved their own self-esteem, whilst supporting their new colleagues' development into the school team. Mentors were also allocated for those experienced assistants attending advanced courses during 2000–01. The programme of induction and mentoring shows how the partners (mentor and mentee) fit their activities into the overall programme. In addition there are some comments from the assistants reflecting on these processes. These appear on the website.

Using team meetings for the dissemination of knowledge became part of a carefully constructed programme of staff development in the school as well. The assistants recognised that when they went out of school to do courses as individuals (the current programme is provided below), there was often much that could be productively shared with colleagues in school. They planned their meetings programme through the term so that on a regular basis a whole meeting was used for staff development and dissemination.

The course attenders also learnt skills of sharing their experiences with colleagues. This again provided a further learning experience, for example in how to concisely and meaningfully impart what they had learnt on a day's course in a one-hour meeting. They became skilled at organising group work and active learning for the other assistants and, where it was felt appropriate, at full staff meetings where they were teaching the teachers as well as the assistants. There is an example on the website of the planning notes for a seminar for the other staff. This did much to confirm to the teaching staff their professional role within the school, although in this school the sense of 'value' existed before the research project began. One of the assistants working in EAL also provided INSET in another school, based on a course she attended at the London Institute of Education. As the deputy head, Sue, said in a note accompanying the evidence about these developments,

> I've enclosed an outline of the training the TAs are delivering to staff at a residential INSET day, 6/4/01. They've organised the content, delivery etc. themselves. What a talented bunch we have!

Park Lane School in Cheshire also recently developed an initiative that involved assistants taking a lead role in the induction training for newly appointed assistants. Dave, the head, described this in the following way:

> within the school development policy the assistants...co-ordinated through the staff development co-ordinator in providing INSET to new members of staff either just before or on arrival in school to take up new posts. These are in several important areas such as handling and lifting and behaviour management.

Vaughan First and Middle School
TRAINING FOR LSAs 2000–2001

INDIVIDUAL TRAINING
• Talk through applications with Sue N. (SENCO)
• Applications to Head for LEA training, daytime and twilight courses
• Courses run outside the LEA applications to the Head
• Long term courses e.g. STA, CLANSA discuss with Sue N. then applications to the Head

LONG TERM COURSES 2000–2001
• Kate Penman – STA September 2000–July 2001
• Lyn McQuater – NVQ Level 3 – Dec 2000 ongoing

COURSES RUN OUTSIDE THE LEA
• Kalpana Sangani – EAL Nov 2000 London Institute

SCHOOL BASED INSET 2000–2001 (All LSAs)
• Social skills (activities and ideas) – Jane Inglese (SACT)
• ICI (for SEN children) – Max Wainwright (Adviser ICT – Harrow)
• Brain Gym – organised by H/T – Harrow TC
• Spelling (strategies to use with SEN groups) – Kerry Hardstaff (A&D team)
• Working with the Speech and Language Therapist – Catherine Thomas (SALT)

VISITS TO SCHOOLS
Visits in pairs to Aylward to observe Social Skills Groups – Summer and Autumn Term 2000
Visits to various schools to observe good practice in SEN and EAL (as appropriate) Spring and Summer term 2001

Parkes Field School in Salford also paid attention to staff development from induction to career structures. Angela, Jane, Tinah and Lynn spent some time considering this in collaboration with their colleagues. A particular area of focus for them was to make sure the most was being made of staff development opportunities and that whatever the assistants had learnt, and any qualifications, certification, etc., should be noted carefully as a record of achievement. They, as a team, then carefully collected evidence of learning, which included additional responsibilities they had taken and learning they had done in school on the job, as well as more formal coursework. This confirmed to them all what a lot they all did know! As one said, 'I'd forgotten I'd done that, I could use it now where I'm working!' Others expressed pride and surprise in a mixture of feelings. They all personalised what became known as their 'professional development portfolios' within an agreed structure of organisation, so that there was a recognised 'house-style' as well. They felt that this record would be useful in the future too, as they applied to take newly defined jobs in the new school, and in respect of a future career structure at school, local and national levels.

Another area the research team addressed was that of professional development interviews. They identified that these needed to be more formalised within the school policy, related to their newly defined job descriptions and also to the portfolios. It was also a time when they were thinking of the new appointments in the new school. In addition they drew up a proforma to prepare themselves for interview which they completed and added to application forms for these new jobs. They wished to be prepared for this as the staffing was being decided in the near future. With the support of Lynn and the management team a new interview schedule was devised and they began to use it within the appraisal structure of the school. This was much appreciated by the assistants themselves and when the Ofsted inspectors were in school they also noted it and approved.

The following comments appear in the Ofsted report:

- All staff have job descriptions, which are reviewed annually.
- The school development plan is effective in raising standards, is very comprehensive, is well linked to targets and regularly monitored. It covers all areas of the school's work, including the professional needs of staff. Staff reviews are regularly carried out and appropriate in-service training is provided for staff as a whole or on an individual basis. For example, all assistants have specialist training and many have had the opportunity, provided by the school, to take additional training such as at National Vocational Qualification level or for Augmentative and Alternative Communication. All staff feel very valued and very much empowered to take on their responsibilities. The results of this can be seen in the quality of their teamwork and their dedication to the pupils and the school.
- All new teaching and non-teaching staff receive well-planned introductory packages. Monitoring and appraisal systems highlight staff training needs and all staff receive regular and ongoing support for their professional development. There are effective induction procedures.

The new job descriptions, portfolios, professional development reviews and new job preparation activities all arose from the fact that at the original workshop the lead researchers had seen the links between the needs for the development of all these activities. They were interwoven tasks each supporting another aspect of the work. The indicator and review questions triggering their action research were those directly related to clear roles and responsibilities and staff development, which they linked together very productively.

There are examples on the website of their preparation for application for jobs in the new school, and revised appraisal interview schedules, with a record of responses, show evidence of the development in thinking and practice that has taken place.

As a result of the action research the **Harrow VI team** also used for the first time a professional development review format devised by the LEA senior officer with responsibility for their work. It had become clear to them during their research activities that this aspect of their professional development was also a service development issue. The support of their senior officer led to them starting a series of interviews with their new team leader Helen. This is in its early stages, but it is already seen as a positive development. Their own appreciation of what they can do has been enhanced by both this initiative and their team meetings. The team feels more intrinsically professional than it did prior to starting the action research, at which point they needed to uncover, discuss and develop their talents. This is exactly what has occurred.

Elizabeth, now working at the RNIB as senior education officer, was also writing training courses for the organisation. This was in addition to the article written in *Visability* about planning processes that many schools and services might well find useful for staff development purposes with their teachers and assistants. She has based much of the course planning on the work that the Harrow team did during the research, feeling that they learnt much from doing it that other teams supporting pupils with visual impairment and their teachers could use and benefit from. Her impression in her new role was that there was much room for development in many LEA teams that she had come to know about, not least in assistants supporting teachers' abilities to provide curriculum access to blind and visually impaired pupils. The in-service training courses she has devised mirror the issues about teamwork, professional development and planning effectively with teachers that the Harrow team undertook. They also draw experienced assistants into the sessions,* where they explain their practice to the participants in the course, illustrating that assistants appreciate learning from one another. There is an example of her planning outline on the website.

Park Lane School in Cheshire has developed performance management targets within professional review activities for assistants as well as for teachers. This was seen as a positive move by the senior management team and the action researchers. The research project work had fitted in well with moves that were already taking place in the school. This was described in a note about their work from the headteacher, Dave:

> regarding the implementation of performance management, the INSET day run by myself and a school consultant did include assistants, resulting in all staff refining the original development objectives that they had, following the annual summer staff reviews with me in July 2000.

In **Harrow**, at **Grange First School** the team set up programmes of in-service training. This included a combination of in-house courses alongside teaching staff, in relation to curriculum development and classroom teamwork. It also involved whole staff meetings working on joint approaches to the literacy strategy, using DfEE guidance to structure the activities. There were also sessions on behaviour management that were structured in a similar way. Joint training of this kind was an innovation for this school. The future plans in a similar vein included IT work. There was also a carefully identified programme of attendance by TAs on LEA and FE external training courses. Evaluation was a key part of this and assistants were encouraged to write reflectively about their experiences on the courses, about what they had gained from them and whether they could usefully share this with the others in the team. This dissemination began to happen during team and staff meetings on a regular basis. Of course, this too was a learning experience for the assistants, putting what they found to be of value to the rest of the team in an accessible way.

The example below illustrates the staff development meeting processes in respect of teachers and assistants working collaboratively in the literacy strategy. The DfEE suggestions were used to construct the discussions and there is a record of the ideas generated during the meeting that was subsequently disseminated to all members of staff in order to support the development of joint classroom practices. There is a record of the issues raised on the website.

GRANGE

**WORKING WITH TEACHING ASSISTANTS – INSET 2
A JOINT TRAINING SESSION FOR TEACHERS AND TEACHING ASSISTANTS
MONDAY, 26TH FEBRUARY 2001, 2–3.30PM**

OBJECTIVE
To develop the role of the Teaching Assistant in the shared section of the Literacy Hour. Teachers and teaching assistants working together in partnership.

AGENDA
2.00–2.20   Review of findings from staff meeting on 22/1/01 – 'Working with teaching Assistants – effective teaching and learning.' Whole group discussion.

2.20–3.00   Introduce the role of the teaching assistant during the shared section of the Literacy Hour.
In year groups look at suggestions from DfEE – develop statements through discussion and shared practice.

Resource management – Early Years team (Beverley, Barbara, Sahira, Tara, Madeline, Sue B, Marion, Sue J)

Oiling the wheels – Year 1 team (Lynne, Norma, Catherine, Mrs Khanna, Varsha, Tracy)

Supervision – Year 2 team (Jo, Leigh, Alison, Nike, Chris, Sharon)

An extra pair of eyes – Year 3 team (Thelma, Linda, Margaret, Linda S, Liz, Paula)

Sue C to join either Year 2 or Year 3 team.

Behaviour Management and Helping the Teaching Assistant role to be discussed by all groups.

Each group to be given large pieces of sugar paper and felt tip pens in order to make a poster relating to the 2 statements under discussion.

3.00–3.30 Feedback and discussion.

As well as the joint staff development meetings the assistants attended, they had their 'own' staff development sessions aimed at sharing their experiences of outside courses with all the assistants in the team. They were encouraged to write their own commentaries or reflections. There are examples on the website of their comments about the courses they attended.

Puss Bank Infants School in Cheshire also focused on professional development from the start of their action research. They – Maggi, the assistant, and Catherine, the learning support coordinator – had felt for some time that there was a lack of appropriate training opportunities locally. (This changed somewhat during the course of the research as key officers were drawn into the research agenda that all of the schools were pursuing.) However, there were in-school developments they felt they were able to make that would go some way to filling in the gaps they perceived in their programmes of staff development, both for individuals and for the team. They carried out an enquiry with all the assistants in the school about each team member's perceptions of the current situation. There are some evaluative comments and suggestions on the website from assistants, about their current opportunities at the time of the review.

Firstly, as a result of this, they initiated a system of professional development review using a format that Catherine adapted from her previous school, Abbey Hills County First School in Morpeth. They also made part of this optional in the first year, the section on the observation of classroom practice. However, the preparation of a self-review and then an interview with the new headteacher, Carl, using the new format, would be expected from all assistants. In addition to this they set targets for the development of training for all TAs.

Devising a professional development portfolio was the other major activity the team undertook. The need to gather evidence of professional achievements, developments, CV and qualifications was seen as important, in preparation for a review grading their sets of responsibilities into levels. The portfolio is structured into a number of sections, using a file in which evidence can be gathered, flexibly enough to meet individual needs and to be personalised in the ways that the assistants choose. The development of this portfolio and that of the professional self-review and review interviews have been linked together in a very productive way. As Maggi said, 'It is so good to be observed and have a discussion about your work. It really helps you think.' The assistants all have a much clearer picture both of their staff development needs for the future and of their achievements from the past.

The professional development framework for teaching assistants is shown below. The interview schedule, classroom observation format and agreements sheet, on the website, all illustrate how the appraisal process developed. The structure of the professional portfolio is also shown.

A network may be established in Macclesfield between the schools involved in the project in order to carry some of this work forward and to meet local needs. Some of the assistants are very experienced and now are able to lead not only their own meetings in areas of expertise but also wider gatherings of staff such as assistants from other schools and in some cases teaching staff as well. **Ryles Park High School** staff have already contributed to LEA staff development meetings and courses, including the secondary induction course from the DfEE. Their deputy headteacher was part of the LEA working group organising these induction sessions, and he quite rightly felt that using the skills of experienced assistants would have great benefits for newly appointed assistants, but also be very good professional development for the Ryles Park assistants themselves. Assistants learning with and from assistants is a positive model of practice that should be replicated more often as they become more confident in their skills.

Puss Bank School

Professional Development Framework for Teaching Assistants

The Initial Discussion

The initial meeting should:

- establish a relaxed but professional climate

- check understanding of Professional Development process

- allow agreement on how information will be gathered (e.g. self review, classroom observation, pupil record sheets)

- establish times and locations of future meetings/observations

Self Review

During the first year of implementation of the Professional Development Framework for Teaching Assistants self-evaluation will consist of a general review questionnaire of five questions which look at your current role, skills you would like to improve and career development. Once the professional development framework is established self evaluation may become more detailed and ask you to look at specific skills related to your job, rating your confidence in each area. As with all professional development documentation the self review is confidential to you and your Team Leader. The targets agreed at the end of the process will need to be shared with the Senior Management Team of the school as part of the wider school development process within the guidelines for confidentiality which exist for all SMT meetings.

Classroom Observations

During the first year of Professional Development for Teaching Assistants classroom observations will be an optional part of the process. All observation times will be agreed with yourself and the class teacher in advance. You can choose whether you want your Team Leader to generally observe your work or focus on a specific aspect of your role. For example, if you have recently undergone training in behaviour management you may want to focus on this area specifically. The observations will be discussed with you at the Development Interview and you will have the opportunity to comment on how well you thought the session went as well as identifying targets for future training.

The Professional Development Interview

The Professional Development Interview should be scheduled to take place after all relevant information has been collected and classroom observations have been completed. The purpose of the meeting is to:

- give feedback based on data collected and observations made

- identify areas for further development

- plan targets and agree how those targets can be met

A record of the discussion will be made for you to keep in your Professional Development Portfolio.

Cont...

Cont...

Target Setting

Targets should form part of the school development process as well as relating to individual development. Between 2 and 5 targets should be set. It is important that all targets are:

Specific – avoid ambiguity
Manageable – no more than 5 and measurable with clear success criteria
Achievable – relate to the individual's experience and expertise available
Realistic
Time related

The post holder and the school share responsibility for the achievement of targets. Progress towards meeting the targets should be reviewed after six months and any changes in circumstances noted. Occasionally outside factors, such as the cancellation of courses, may prevent targets being met and alternative ways of developing skills may need to be discussed.

The Professional Development Portfolio

Copies of all documentation completed as part of the Professional Development process should be kept in your portfolio along with a record of any development activities completed during the year.

Reference: Contents of Professional Development Portfolios for Classroom Assistants/ Teaching Assistants.

Internal career structures is also an issue in several of the other research schools. At least three of them already had senior assistants at the start of the research, with pay that matched that seniority, allocated from school budgets, through an internal decision-making process. They had no more funding proportionally than many schools that have not done this, but senior management saw it as a priority to recognise these assistants.

At the time of writing there are several schools that, through appraisal or professional development interviews and the preparation of portfolios, have now collected considerable evidence in support of recognising senior status for assistants. They are likely to make internal decisions to promote some assistants in recognition of their achievements, experience, responsibilities and qualifications, whether or not a national framework can be used in support of them during 2002.

This then, has been an examination of various forms of professional development from induction to career structures undertaken by the schools doing action research using the indicators of effective practice. The work has clearly had a major impact on the professional lives of the assistants directly involved in the research. But it has also reached beyond them to impact on the learning of their colleague assistants, the class teachers and learning support coordinators, senior managers and governors. It has also helped them to work more effectively in support of the school, the curriculum, the teachers and, crucially, the pupils they work with in the classroom. As they have developed skills and confidence, so the pupils have benefited.

Section 4
Summary: reflections on future practice development

13 Working effectively with teaching assistants

This chapter summarises some of the most important points and ideas, key strategies and experiences that have led to the recommendations about developing practice in this book. It does this in two ways. Firstly, it concludes with the most significant lessons learnt through the original study and the pilot research that followed it. Secondly, it uses the words of the assistants who worked as lead researchers and some of their colleagues in school to provide 'illuminative insights' for the reader.

This rich and varied data obtained is at times reflective and offers a critique of the overall approach. However, there is also a real sense of what being action researchers meant to the assistants. It does this not least in terms of their self-esteem, feelings of value and appreciation, but also their self-advocacy within their working contexts (and in some cases, beyond their own team and into wider scenarios).

It is also important to acknowledge that, as in our original research findings, there are two very notable dimensions that we should mention. Firstly, there is the enthusiasm and lack of cynicism that exists in many assistants across the country. Despite the fact that at the time we were directly involved in both pieces of research, there was no formal career or pay structure assistants still maintained levels of enthusiasm and commitment that are a credit to them. Secondly, where schools demonstrate in a variety of ways, not least senior managers' understanding and support for their work, that TAs are valued, great things can happen. Clearly, now that there is to be a national structure for career development, all their commitment and enthusiasm is more likely to be rewarded.

This changing national context with all three government strategies in place (good practice guidance, national induction training for both primary and secondary assistants and a qualifications and competencies framework) should lead to more consistency in practice across the country. This may well replicate some of the excellent practice that already exists in some settings, and that is described in this book.

Significant lessons for future practice development

The action research described in the book has strategic implications for others. The analysis provided in Chapter 6 is key to these. In using indicators of effective practice and review questions to carry out the action research there was no doubt that in a sense the ideas that came from our original research in producing those indicators have been truly tested. What has become evident is the way they can be used flexibly and that they are not seen by those using them as a set of instructions. Instead they can be used as a tool for review and development that takes account, from the beginning, of the individual starting points and needs of any particular setting.

However, some patterns emerged for the settings that took part in the action research which provide potentially useful guidance to others. Some of the key aspects of the work that resulted in the success of their projects are outlined below.

The role of assistants was examined very closely, and effectively, through:

- a focus on job descriptions, flexible deployment and management practices in respect to these;
- staff development opportunities and induction processes.

The key issues for management were

- senior teaching staff and school leaders developing awareness of the issues identified within the indicators of effective practice;
- an appreciation of the need to change management practices;
- resulting developments in both policy and practice.

In addition important factors within the action research were:

- a senior member of staff strategically fulfilling a leadership and advocacy role;
- this role kept the 'voice' of the action researchers on agendas for staff meetings and in discussions with key groups of people such as senior managers or governors;
- self-advocacy generated by both the lead researcher assistants and the whole teams of assistants has placed them firmly at the forefront of staff and practice development and school improvement. The lead that assistants took at the national dissemination conferences was impressive, their appreciative audiences applauding them and their presentations, their confidence and their work. Listeners were impressed with the accounts of the development of confidence and self-esteem that came from their involvement in action research. The assistants are rightly proud of these achievements.

Assistants' views and reflections

These reflections demonstrate the worth that assistants placed on the developments in which they were playing a key role. The set of reflections here is drawn from reflective comments that appeared in the project evaluation report of December 2000 and are a compilation of unsigned writing. There are some extended reflective pieces on the website.

> The LSA project has increased my confidence in others and myself and hopefully they in me. It has given me hope that there will come a day when there's a nationwide recognition of the role LSAs play in our children's education and an appropriate career structure is formed as a result.
>
> It has brought us closer together, I feel, as a whole school team developing a greater understanding and a renewed respect of the part we each play to make our school a success as recently confirmed by the positive feedback from our Ofsted inspection.

> I think being involved in the restructuring our job descriptions was a very valuable exercise. It clearly shows when put down on paper just how flexible and hardworking we are. Not only for ourselves, but also for outsiders and people looking at support work as a career.
>
> Putting together my personal profile was good. It has given me confidence in my own abilities and I have something to show and be proud of. It helps show the direction my training and careers are going e.g. strengths, weaknesses etc. I believe it gives ideal opportunities for our staff to share individual ideas, expertise and brought us together as a team. I really hope this project helps in some way to build better career prospects in the future.

> In conclusion I would say that the project has brought our school's LSAs together – but without isolating us from other team members i.e. teachers, SMT. Instead it has brought all the school together in raising an awareness of our role through our practice job description and Personal Development Profiles. This along with the motivation it has inspired has increased my willingness to learn and develop new skills to promote my career. The results of this will reflect in the most important part of my role as an LSA to give the children I work with the best possible care and education. After all this is a job I love!!

> The LSA project has made staff, especially senior staff, more aware of our role in school. More liaison between staff and LSAs takes place. Set time is put aside on the timetable once a fortnight for the whole team and the Senco where we talk through any difficulties and plan any programmes etc. As a result of the project the team are more enthusiastic and trying new things in the department.

> For me an important aspect of being involved...the opportunity to meet with the others in the visual impairment team...These regular meetings have, I believe, had several positive effects. They have increased the cohesiveness of the team; given us an opportunity to share working practice; provided a platform for new ideas, some of which sound extremely enterprising (!) and given us an insight into the ideas an enlightened team leadership is trying to incorporate into LEA thinking.

The team's discussions on the project focused us together that we should strive to ensure that the children within our service are as independent as possible by providing best access, thus developing their self-esteem, social awareness and confidence. In this respect, from my experience, class teachers are encouraged and grateful for the planning with the LSA and specialist teacher which gives them more confidence with the disabled pupil and the feedback from the lessons is constructive.

I have felt very positive about the outcomes of our research. It has confirmed for me that we do achieve good practice and increased my confidence in feeling justified in pursuing that aim. Although I already knew planning was vital, I still felt apologetic, sometimes for having to insist on this requirement from the class teachers whom I knew were under enormous pressure.

S and myself went to the management board meeting at school and outlined to senior staff, the head and governors the aims and objectives of the project. We were well received and asked to attend another meeting. We did this on 6th June. It was noticeable that the head (who is very supportive of all his staff), listened very intently to what we had to say... I mentioned that as a progression from 'in-class support' it might be an idea to have 'specialist' LSAs in departments... we suggested geography and maths for starters (having discussed this with colleagues in learning support and the already good working relationships with these faculties).

So far the use of the indicator 'LSAs work cooperatively with teachers to support the learning and participation of pupils', has been carried out at W school by S and myself with excellent results.

In conclusion, I would just like to add that as a result of our presentation to management board, many staff members have been approaching S and myself and asking questions and showing an interest. A copy of the minutes from management board are circulated to the teaching staff following each meeting.

Hopefully it will make a tremendous difference to all concerned. When the policy is introduced in school it will give clear guidelines to teaching staff as to how and when to use their support. It will also allow the LSAs to know exactly what is required of them.

The introduction of this policy will hopefully make way for termly or half-termly meetings between teachers and LSAs, which can only be of benefit to both parties involved. None more than the LSAs as most times you can feel very isolated and appear to be pestering when questioning what it is the teacher wants you to do.

I hope that the teachers who are not used to having support in their classroom realise that we are there to support the children and not to intimidate them. I know some members of staff feel under pressure with another person in their classroom.

I hope the project will allow me to be seen as a whole member of the classroom and not just someone who is only there part of the time. I hope it will give teachers a clearer picture on what is their role when working with an LSA or any form of support worker and what they can reasonably ask us to do when working with the children.

In the short time that the school has been involved in the project we have become much more aware of our roles in school. It has prompted our LSA team to look very closely at our existing job descriptions and it was decided that they needed to be rewritten. Plans were also started towards the writing of an induction policy for non-teaching staff, this will be a new policy. This was a great opportunity to work as a team on two very important documents.

The induction package: the group started brainstorming their thoughts and ideas about what should be included. The group found it difficult to keep to the matter in hand as they wanted to share their own experiences as new staff. However, we were able to draw up a list, including: 'a mentor to show new staff round the school and answer any questions in the first weeks/months; staff to share and meet and discuss common ground to ensure consistency for the pupils; some training and information on specific special needs; a meeting with the classteacher to discuss pupils' needs and how best the classteacher and support staff can work together.'

I feel sure the management team will look carefully at our suggestions and an induction package for support staff will be next on the agenda.

The job descriptions review: it was an enjoyable challenge – listing the various jobs we all do, a whittling them down to what was more a general description to fit in the job description. Whilst working on these ideas another role we felt was necessary to be included in our new job descriptions was that of mentoring of new staff, this opened up the issue of induction. Our own experiences were that none had felt that they had anyone in particular to turn to or to be shown properly around the school and all felt that having a mentor would have been very useful.

Concluding remarks

The reflections above illustrate the value of doing this kind of development work from the assistants' perspectives. Furthermore they demonstrate the messages about inclusive practice with assistants that should be heard by any schools wishing to develop more inclusive practice with their pupils. Where the assistants feel as included as these, the likelihood is that the pupils they support will also feel that they are fully included in the classroom and school learning environment.

In offering the materials in the book we feel that there is much here to support the work of others. What has been done in the schools and services described is not offered on the basis of being the 'perfect solutions' to the needs of other schools and LEAs. The materials here are the results of focused action research undertaken in individual contexts. Each of these contexts had different starting points and needs, some more 'advanced' than others, for the development of their practice. Therefore, the materials displayed in the text and appendices and on the website are not 'perfect', but merely those schools' and services' best efforts at seeking their own ways forward. Thus they are given away by those assistants and their teaching colleagues in the spirit of collegiality and in the hope that others will gain both inspiration and practical ideas through them. We hope they will be received and appreciated in that spirit.

What the book does provide, however, besides the generosity of our colleagues in the action research settings in offering illustrative materials, is some strategic advice that should indeed be usable (even 'generalisable') in many school and LEA contexts. Using this advice in conjunction with the Good Practice Guide 'Working with Teaching Assistants' should lead to an acknowledgement of what is already good practice in a particular setting and how to build on that. As authors we conclude by saying that it has been a privilege to work with those colleagues who have given their thoughts, inspiration, time and efforts to enable us to write this book.

Appendix 1
Pen pictures of the participant schools and services

Cheshire LEA

Puss Bank School: Catherine Mattocks, Maggi Simmons

This primary school is in Macclesfield and is a newly combined infant and junior school with a nursery and assessment base, involving additional provision for special needs. It has enhanced numbers of TAs because of this. At the start of the research project the infant school was originally involved.

Upton Priory Junior School: Ann Parr, Karen Woodall, Kath Sayers, Kath Everitt

This primary school is in Macclesfield and is additionally resourced to take pupils with physical disabilities. There is a substantial team of TAs in the school.

Park Lane School: Helen Chadwick, Pat Redding
This school is in Macclesfield and is a special school for about 40 pupils aged two to 19. It has a substantial number of TAs, some of which are LEA additional staff for named pupils. The pupils have additional needs that range from profound and multiple learning difficulties to autistic spectrum disorders.

Ryles Park High School: Rosemary Bamford, Sam Hulme, Carolyn Ashcroft
This high school is in Macclesfield and is additionally resourced to provide an inclusive setting for pupils who might otherwise be in special provision and 110 of whom have a statement. It has a substantial team of TAs, funded by the LEA and the school itself.

Officers: Fintan Bradley, David Richards

Harrow LEA

Grange First School: Lynne Sumner, Brenda Gibson, Sharon Smith
This three-form entry first school has an increasing team of full- and part-time assistants employed on a variety of contracts. It was in part because of this development that the school chose to join the research.

Vaughan Nursery, First and Middle School: Sue Nilsson, Surinder Minhas, Jackie Millington
This school has a substantial team of 15 full- and part-time assistants and is a two-form entry school. The assistants are funded to support both general learning and individual special needs on a variety of contracts.

Visual Impairment Sensory and Communication team: Elizabeth Clery, Janice Allen, Rosie Downing, Jaquie Lawrence, Kathryn Lees, Margaret Banger
This team is part of Harrow's central support services. It supports the inclusion of blind and partially sighted pupils in mainstream primary and secondary schools. There are advisory teachers and TAs in the team.

Whitmore High School: Karen White, Anne Perring, Sneha Radia, Angie Lawrence
This secondary school has a long tradition of first integrated and now inclusive practice in Harrow. It is additionally resourced for pupils with significant additional needs who might otherwise be in specialist provision. There is a substantial team of assistants in the school, some of whom are directly resourced by the school, others by the LEA.

Officers: Jackie Harrop, Elaine Gardner

Salford LEA

Parkes Field School: Lynn Monks, Angela Macdonald, Jane Walsh, Tinah Clarey
This was a school for primary aged pupils with physical and/or multiple difficulties at the start of the research. It has been amalgamated with two others into a completely new school, **Springwood**, since then. There was a substantial TA team, many of whom are now on the new school staff.

Moorside High School: Dave Winning, Marie Sinclair, Yvonne Gibson
This is a secondary school that was the first in Salford to be resourced with assistants as part of its provision of in-class support. It now has a substantial team of assistants.

Primary Partnership Service: Yvette Wright, Sarah Lindley, Linda Sales
This service provides educational support to 18 Key Stage One and Two pupils who have experienced permanent exclusion or are at risk of this, due to emotional, behavioural and social needs. The centre offers part-time placements and reintegration support. There is a team of assistants who work with the teachers in the service to provide this support.

Officer: Judith Jones

N.B. As was stated in the introduction to the book, many other people in each setting were involved in the action research. These names are those of the 'lead researchers'.

Appendix 2

Indicators of effective practice with learning support assistants

Joint Manchester University and LEA pilot research

Project outline agreed in principle with LEA personnel

Stage One

Initial phase: December 1999 – January 2000
- **Meeting with key LEA personnel to define scope of project in the LEA:**
  - Defining aims for LEA's project and broad foci/targets within these.
  - Identifying participants – LEA and school (service managers and teaching staff, LSAs, school managers (possibly Sencos *if* they are SMT members), teachers and LSAs, maybe governors and parents).
  - Defining criteria for school participation, one from each of primary, special and secondary and one 'service-base' in the LEA, i.e. four 'sites' each selecting at least two personnel, one of whom should be a senior manager.
  - Setting dates for LEA-based workshop meeting and timeline for school and LEA visits by researchers from Manchester University.

Next phase: January – May 2000
- **Research workshop for all LEA and school participants**
  - Led by Maggie Balshaw and Peter Farrell with LEA staff in support.
  - Defining the task overall and in each 'base' – LEA/schools.
  - Drawing up an action research plan for consultation and implementation in each base. Setting dates for Manchester University researchers to visit each school/base for half a day to support 'work-in-progress', and gather initial data from participants on developments so far.
  - Agreeing (broadly) the format of written evidence in preparation for the first evaluation workshop (June 2000)
- **School visits by Manchester University researchers**
  - 'Work-in-progress' discussions and support

Third phase: June 2000
- **Joint initial evaluation workshop with three LEAs**
  - Prior to this preparation of evidence which informs the debate on how the indicators and review questions are working in practice.

- Gathering evidence through evaluation workshop presentations from each LEA and written or other evidence chosen by personnel from the LEA and its schools.
- Devise how to proceed from here, both these LEAs and others (who might well send at least one representative to join the day).

Date set for workshop: June 28th 2000, at Manchester University

Stage Two

June 2000 – Easter 2001
- Continuing research and evaluation with redefined review questions and other LEA participants, using when available, funding from whatever source we have been able to secure.

December 1999

Appendix 3
Indicators of effective practice and choices made by project participants

Framework for evaluating practice at all levels

A. Role	B. Management	C. Training
A.1 LSAs work co-operatively with teachers to support the learning and participation of pupils	B.l Teachers' management strategies provide clear guidance as to how LSAs should work in their classrooms	C.l Teachers and LSAs learn together to improve the quality of their work
A.2 LSAs work with teachers to prepare lesson plans and materials	B.2 Schools have policies outlining roles and responsibilities of LSAs	C.2 School staff development programmes foster the competence of LSAs and teachers to carry out their respective tasks
A.3 LSAs contribute to the evaluation of the outcomes of lessons	B.3 LEA policies ensure that LSAs' conditions of employment foster effective practice	C.3 LEAs provide relevant additional training and support for LSAs
A.4 LSAs make relevant contributions to wider school activities		C.4 Use is made of (institution based) external courses to extend the expertise of LSAs

Which indicators were chosen? (*indicators chosen by schools/services)

	A.1 **	B.1 **	C.1 *
	A.2 **	B.2 *******	C.2 ***
	A.3 **	B.3	C.3 *
	A.4		C.4 *
Totals	**6 from A**	**9 from B**	**6 from C**
	Role	Management	Training

Source: from P. Farrell *et al.* (1999) *The Management, Role and Training of Learning Support Assistants*. London: DfEE Publications

Appendix 4
Workshop activities

These activity sheets appear in the order in which they were used, moving from classroom practice to policy development.

GPG Indicator 3.1: sample questions for discussion

Creating partnerships with teachers

Indicator 3.1 TAs work cooperatively with teachers to support the learning and participation of pupils

- Do TAs understand the purpose of lesson activities?

- Do TAs share in long- and medium-term planning?

- Are TAs involved in flexible decision-making about plans during lessons?

- Do TAs and teachers plan in ways that demonstrate to pupils their commitment to teamwork?

Make some notes about your school's current practice and the above questions
Be ready to discuss these issues with colleagues

GPG Indicator 2.2: sample questions for discussion

Providing flexible deployment

Indicator 2.2 The expertise, skills and knowledge of TAs is used flexibly to foster the learning of pupils

- Are TAs' previous experiences and skills used to support curriculum access and flexible approaches?

- Is the particular curricular knowledge of TAs recognised and used?

- Is care taken to make sure that TAs are actively encouraged to work in curriculum areas in which they feel confident and interested?

Make some notes about your school's current practice and the above questions
Be ready to discuss these issues with colleagues

GPG Indicator 1: sample questions for discussion

Defining responsibilities clearly

Indicator 1 Schools have clear policies outlining the roles and responsibilities of TAs

- Does the school provide appropriate job descriptions for TAs?

- Does the school involve TAs in drawing up the job descriptions?

- Do the job descriptions reflect a balance of responsibilities, reflecting TAs' support to teachers, the curriculum, pupils and the school?

- Are TAs given time within their contracts for preparation, meetings, other administrative tasks and training?

- Does the school's staff development plan target the needs of teachers and managers in understanding their role in managing TAs?

Make some notes about your school's current practice and the above questions
Be ready to discuss these issues with colleagues

GPG Indicator 6: sample questions for discussion

Reviewing performance and development

Indicator 6 TAs are supported in relation to their induction, mentoring and development needs

- Are TAs provided with a school induction programme?

- Are job descriptions reviewed with TAs on a regular basis?

- Are TAs encouraged to complete a professional achievement and development portfolio?

- Does the school structure responsibilities for TAs to reflect their qualifications, experience and training?

Make some notes about your school's current practice and the above questions
Be ready to discuss these issues with colleagues

Appendix 5
School and service action research plans

WHITMORE HIGH

Action Research plan

Key people involved	Department
Janice Howkins	Head of Learning Development Department
Karen White	Teacher of History and English; member of Learning Development Department
Angie Lawrence	Parent-Governor at Whitmore High School
Sneha Radia	Learning Support Assistant
Anne Perring	Learning Support Assistant
Seri March	Head of Geography Department
Clive Davis	Teacher of Mathematics

Targets

As a team at Whitmore we decided to focus on the Maths and Geography Departments as Sneha Radia and Anne Perring had direct links with these departments. It was felt 'unworkable' to focus on more than two departments; although Sneha Radia and Karen White began putting the team's ideas directly into practice when Sneha was timetabled to support Karen's Year 8 History class after the Easter holidays.

The areas we focused on were:

- A1 – LSAs work co-operatively with teachers to support the learning and participation of pupils
- A2 – LSAs work with teachers to prepare lesson plans and materials
- A3 – LSAs contribute to the evaluation of outcomes of lessons

The first thing that took place after the initial meeting at the Teachers' Centre was that Sneha and Anne went to the Management Board Meeting at school and outlined to senior staff, the Head and Governors the aims and objectives of the project. Meetings were then held with Seri March, Head of Geography and Clive Davis, Teacher of Maths to discuss the focus areas that the team had decided to focus on.

It was decided that the following strategies should be used as a starting point for discussion between the LSAs and teaching staff.

- Identification of students' needs in conjunction with their IEPs
- Sight of lesson plans and discussion
- Agreement regarding differentiation of tasks e.g worksheets
- General discussion of effective use of LSA in lessons

The initial meeting with teaching staff was very positive. Individual students' needs were discussed and longer-term plans regarding the subject content of lessons were touched upon. A second meeting was planned where teaching staff would be asked to answer specific questions based on the issues detailed in the Review Agenda for Dimension A: Roles. A meeting was then held between Sneha Radia, Anne Perring and Karen White, where a questionnaire was designed specifically around the Dimension A: Roles issues.

The questionnaire was distributed to Seri March and Clive Davis. Karen White also completed the questionnaire. The results illustrated that there were specific areas which could be developed (see questionnaires) such as LSAs were not involved in the planning of lessons.

Indicators of Effective Practice with Learning Support Assistants
Upton Priory Junior School   June 2000

Project plan

The targets are:
- To create a relevant job description.
- To provide a structure for management of LSAs.
- To set up regular review meetings.

The purpose is:
- To develop a greater awareness of the LSA role.
- To contribute to overall staff development and school improvement.

The people involved:
- The senior management (head and deputy), to oversee the project.
- The Special Educational Needs Co-ordinator, to run the project, to write the report with the assistance of the Senior LSA.
- The Learning Support Assistants, to discuss the job descriptions and the extent of their role.
- The teaching staff, to consider the role of the LSAs and the impact of this on their teaching strategies.

The time scale is:
- Job description: Summer term 2000.
- Management structure: Autumn term 2000.
- Role awareness: Autumn term 2000.

Progress so far...

- After the introductory workshop programme, we met with the senior management and explained the overall project to them. We discussed our focus on the management issues outlined in section B2 and they agreed that this would be a good starting point.
- We had a good meeting with Maggie Balshaw and all the LSAs. We outlined the project and our particular focus and all agreed that this was a priority which would underpin further discussion and progress. Maggie encouraged us to consider various aspects of our jobs under the headings Rewarding, Challenging and Stressful.
- Rewarding aspects include:
  - A sense of achievement in enabling a child to gain learning/physical independence.
  - Working as a team.
  - Good relationships with child/parents/teacher.
  - Residential visits.
- Challenging aspects include:
  - Working with behavioural problems.
  - Working with a new child, recognising skills/needs and developing these.
  - Organising work with small groups.
  - Motivating and holding a child's interest.

- Developing confidence in particular skills, e.g. swimming.
- Delivering the Additional Literacy Strategy.
- Getting teaching staff to take notice of the child.
- A lack of consistency of approach by the teaching staff.
- Being included in games and dancing.
- Residential trips.
- Stressful aspects include:
  - Not always knowing in advance what is happening in the lessons.
  - Frequent changes of instructions at short notice.
  - Not having enough time to do essential regular activities, e.g. physiotherapy.

The main issues to emerge from this discussion
- Communication.
- Consistency.

- At their next meeting, the LSAs began to discuss the job description. They discussed the various aspects of their role and looked at some examples of job descriptions (see Appendix 7) to see how their role might best be outlined. At an INSET day in July, we hope to bring all this thinking together to write the job description, to plan how to discuss the role with teaching staff, particularly the communication and consistency issues and how to address the issue of management structure and support.

Ann Parr and Karen Woodall.

Manchester Project action plan (extract)

TASK	BY WHOM	BY WHEN	OUTCOMES
6. For Maggie Balshaw to meet with: • Headteacher • SEN Support Team To raise awareness of the Project.	Maggie Balshaw – delivered Sue Nilsson – organised	29th March 2000	Positively accepted. Headteacher and Team raised their awareness
7. To brief staff: • outline project • talk about indicators • ask for support • how it can benefit all	Sue Nilsson	April 2000 (so late due to OFSTED)	Received positively and would give help, support, fill in questionnaires etc.

8. Look at:
• Job Descriptions and redraft in light of LSAs' roles
• Use indicators to measure effectiveness of Job Description "B2".
	SEN Support Team
	2 working parties
	  i. LSAs supporting individual pupils;
	  ii. LSAs support classes and having welfare as dual role.
		1/2 DAY INSET
		26th May 2000
			1. Group 1 found task easiest as their role was more specific – used Handbook for Learning Support Assistants.
			2. Group 2 found task more difficult as they were trying to include their varied role into 1 job description.

9. Questionnaires compiled and given out to staff using indicators: Ref: A2 – 1, 2, 4, 5, 6 A3 – 1, 2, 3, 4 B1 – 1, 2 B2 – 3, 4, 7, 10 C2 – 1, 2, 3 • 1 questionnaire – teaching staff. • 1 questionnaire with additions to LSAs.	Team and SENCO	May/June 2000	Awaiting results

PARKES FIELD

Area(s) chosen and why:

Following the Introductory Workshop we made a brief evaluation of the three main areas of practice:

1. Classroom practice and activities,
2. Staff development,
3. Management.

We chose management as an appropriate area for development in our school. We decided it would be beneficial to create a clearer structure to the role of the LSA to make it more effective within the school.

On return to school, and after discussion with the Head Teacher, three targets were identified within the **management** area. The targets were as follows:

1. To involve the LSAs in drawing up new job descriptions and to review them annually.
2. To review and restructure the policy document on the role of the LSA.
3. To foster professional development through the introduction of a staff profile, recording evidence of positive achievement.

Through these we set out to do the following:

- clarify the roles and responsibilities of the LSAs
- ensure that conditions of employment foster positive staff development
- improve the quality of the service to pupils
- promote effective working practice within the classroom.

Learning Support Assistant Project: First Meeting   **2.3.00**

Purpose: to feedback to Headteacher detail and content of LSA Project Workshop.
Present: A.W.D., L.M., and A.M.

- Informed Headteacher of project.
- Passed on written information.
- Discussed ideas for our project i.e. LSA Personal Profile.
- Headteacher very supportive.
- Discussed LSA job description and roles.
- Discussed ways of approaching the project with involvement of staff.

Proposals:

1. To meet up with staff and inform them of project.
2. Listen to general feedback.
3. Give out copies of Workshop sheets and information.
4. Ask staff to brainstorm i.e. go away and write down what they actually do in practical terms.
5. Profiles voluntary?
6. Discuss in Class Teams the following week.
7. Plan another meeting to discuss 'Record of Achievement' or 'Profile'.
8. Discuss headings and format of profile e.g. Plastic wallets, file. User friendly.
9. Arrange time to update and discuss job description.
10. Involve Care Assistants in care team to add another point of view.
11. Discuss with staff – times for carrying out work.

Action Research Plan (Continued)

We chose to base our project on the indicators and review questions identified in the DfEE research report 161 completed by the Manchester group. The following are examples of some of these.

LSA Management

B1 Teachers/management strategies provide clear guidance as to how LSAs should work in the classroom.
Issues to consider:

• Are teachers familiar with the job description of LSAs?
Before the project: Teachers were aware that LSAs had a job description and that they could refer to it if necessary.
Since project: LSAs here at Parkes Field School have been involved in drawing up new job descriptions as part of this project. As LSAs we wrote details of our role which we then discussed together with teaching staff at our class team meetings. This meant all were aware of the content, structure and format etc. From this it developed into a whole school objective through staff meetings and class team meetings making all staff aware of the LSA role, that everybody had had an opportunity to discuss and make contributions to. (See Appendix – Job Description)

B2 Schools have policies outlining the roles and responsibilities of LSAs.
• Do schools have clearly defined criteria for use in appointing LSAs?
Issues to consider:
A copy of the criteria is given with the job description which is issued with the application form. Specific criteria is also used for different roles within the school, e.g. Communication Officer, VI Intervenor, NVQ Assessor, all roles taken by LSAs

• Do schools provide appropriate job descriptions for LSAs?
Part of our project was to update and restructure the LSA job description of the LSA at Parkes Field School. The format and contents were put together by LSAs, brought to class teams, and then the whole school for discussion. The Headteacher then used the LSA suggested headings and contents to draw up a new general job description. Following this each LSA had the opportunity to 'personalise' their job description by adding additional responsibilities, skills and duties, making it more individual and also to distinguish roles.
(See B1 above and Appendix – Job description also.)

• Are job descriptions reviewed on a regular basis?
Since the project all LSAs have an individual (personalised) job description which can be updated and have additional training/skills etc. added when necessary. This is an advantage of having an individual job description as well as a standard/general copy.
(See Appendix – Job Description.)

Continued...

HARROW VI TEAM

Four LSAs who currently work in four different schools (primary and secondary) across the LEA to support the learning of pupils who are educationally blind, the Resources Co-ordinator for large print and braille and the Advisory Teacher (Visual Impairment) constitute the group working on this project. An initial look at the indicators suggested that a number of them would be very appropriate for use within our chosen focus of the planning process. These are:

A1. LSAs work co-operatively with teachers to support the learning and participation of pupils;

A2. LSAs work with teachers to prepare lesson plans and materials;

B1. Teachers' management strategies provide clear guidance as to how LSAs should work in their classrooms;

C1. Teachers and LSAs learn together to improve the quality of their work.

Research Plan

• To analyse the different stages of the planning process and to establish the methods used to put these into practice. (April 2000)

▼

• To validate our findings with the pupils. (June 2000)

▼

• To share our approach to planning with others, including those within the four schools and to a wider audience across the borough. (Different times depending on method of dissemination but mainly September 2000 onwards)

Outcomes

Focus group established   (4 LSAs, Resources Co-ordinator for large print/braille) facilitated by Advisory Teacher (Visual Impairment)

▼

Meeting (1) – Initial discussion on planning principles/practice.

▼

Meeting (2)
• LSAs and Resources Co-ordinator each brought a flow chart of their planning process (Appendix 1) including potential difficulties/barriers.
• Drew out common aspects and differences between schools in primary/secondary phase and devised planning chart suitable for (a) primary schools (b) high schools. (Appendix 2.)
• Facilitator wrote up a report about work to date and main findings and included planning charts → to be published in Learning Support Newsletter (to be distributed to all LEA schools).
• Preliminary discussion on testing findings with pupils – how this should be done.

▼

Meeting (3)
• Organised date/format for discussion group.
• Planned reports for Manchester Conference

▼

Meeting (4)

- Four pupils met – this opportunity used as a vehicle not only to test out how planning/preparation works for them but to gain other information about school life in general. Group led by oldest pupil (aged 16) others aged 12, 11, 9, without adult intervention (meeting taped).
- Wrote up summary based on key findings.

This process has offered opportunities for in-depth analysis and reflection which are not generally available. It has been very positive for all involved and each has benefited by being part of the process. All our thinking has moved on and for the LSAs who are working in this field it has been very supportive.

PUSS BANK

Action Research Plan
Aims
To improve training opportunities for Learning Support Assistants within Puss Bank Infant School through:
> i. the establishment of a programme of staff development interviews with annual targets set for training and development.
> ii. The identification and use of training opportunities for support staff through attendance at courses, INSET programmes and other development activities.

Selection of the indicators and review questions from the Manchester/DfEE Study
We looked again at the framework for evaluating practice given in the Manchester/ DfEE Report and selected Dimension C (Training) as our area of research focusing in on point C2. This contained the following questions:
C2. Training
School development plans foster the competence of Learning Support Assistants and teachers to carry out their respective tasks.

Issues to consider:
i. Are Learning Support Assistants currently provided with a school induction programme?
ii. Is there a programme of staff development for Learning Support Assistants?
iii. Do Learning Support Assistants participate in wider staff development activities?
iv. Are LSAs given direct support in developing aspects of their classroom practice?
v. Does the school development programme include attention to the skills of teachers and managers working with LSAs?
vi. Are opportunities for LSA staff development offered during paid work time?
vii. Are LSAs given staff development opportunities in relation to career progression?

Reference
Farrell, P., Balshaw, M., Polat, F. (1999) *The Management, Role and Training of Learning Support Assistants.* page 70

A time line of targets and outcomes was prepared for the Spring and Summer terms and an initial questionnaire was written to gauge opinion regarding training opportunities for support staff. This focused on 3 of the questions identified in the Manchester/DfEE report namely;
ii. Is there a programme of staff development for Learning Support Assistants?
iii. Do Learning Support Assistants participate in wider staff development activities?
iv. Are LSAs given direct support in developing aspects of their classroom practice?

Identification of school staff to be involved in the project

On our return to school two initial meetings were held to share information from the workshop. Catherine fed back to the Senior Management Team and Maggi fed back to the Learning Support Assistants working in the three departments within the school. Eleven people were identified as likely to benefit from a programme of professional development for support staff. Maggi Simmons held an initial briefing meeting to share information regarding the Manchester Study. The following staff were invited to attend:

| Pauline Trueman | mainstream nursery |
| Shirley Dawson | |

Jane Nash	ASD group
Jane Williams	
Lisa Caudwell	

| Lesley Copestick | Assessment Unit |
| Sally Evans | |

| Lynn Avery | Infant MLD group |

| Joy Wood | mainstream infant school |
| Julie | |

Catherine Mattocks briefed the Senior Management Team of the school regarding the March workshop and Manchester Study. This meeting involved:

Sandy Blythe	Headteacher
Terry Kennedy	Deputy Headteacher
Sally Ancell	Head of Foundation Stage

Copies of information regarding the project were also given to Lynette Cookson, Chair of Governors.

Time line of targets and outcomes
Spring and Summer Term 2000

1. Catherine Mattocks and Maggi Simmons to attend 1 day workshop on the Management, Role and Training of Learning Support Assistants led by Dr Peter Farrell and Dr Maggie Balshaw. (13th March 2000)
2. Action research area selected by Catherine and Maggi during workshop. (13th March 2000)
3. Catherine to feedback to SMT at next available Meeting. (March 2000)
4. Maggi to arrange feedback meeting to Learning Support Assistants. (March 2000)
5. Action Research Statement, linked to a Personal Development Programme for Learning Support Assistants produced. (April 2000)
6. Focus group, with a representative from each department in school, to meet with Dr Maggie Balshaw. (May/June 2000)
7. Feedback to Senior Management Team on 22nd May.
8. Catherine and Maggi prepare draft report for the conference to be held at Manchester University 28th June 2000.
9. Draft Reports circulated to Area Office (Copy to Fintan Bradley/Dave Richards) (July 2000)
10. Guidance issued to Support Staff in school regarding the contents of their record of professional development/professional portfolios. (July 2000)
11. Questionnaire to be issued to teachers using as its framework the interview schedule for mainstream teachers given in the Manchester/DfEE report. (Page 90) (July 2000)

Time line of targets and outcomes
Autumn 2000 onwards

NB: timings and content are provisional and will be subject to discussion with and agreement by the new Headteacher who is due to take up their post in January 2001.

What next?

1. Draft professional development package produced linked to Investors in People and school training days and presented to SMT/Governors.
   (Autumn 2000)
2. Support Staff to start to put together personal portfolios from information currently available.
   (September/October 2000)
3. Responses to teacher questionnaire analysed and areas for training noted.
   (September 2000)
4. Look at priorities for training and discuss feasibility of setting up a training day on one of these issues using local speakers.
   (October 2000)
5. Identify and contact schools/organisations to link with for training.
   (October 2000)
6. Identify and contact possible sources of funding.
   (October 2000)
7. Decide on time scale for initial interviews with all support staff.
   (November 2000)
8. Decide on format of preparatory task using information gathered from other schools as a guide.
   (March/April 2001)
9. Individual development interviews held with all support staff with targets for development set for 2001/2002.
   (April/May 2001)

Appendix 6
Examples of questionnaires based on the Manchester Report indicators and review questions

VAUGHAN

Questionnaire in the management, role and training of LSAs

LSA responses (12 returned questionnaires out of 15)	*YES*	*NO*
1. Are you involved in discussion of longer term plans?	5	7
2. Do you take part in planning lessons?	8 s/times	4
3. Do you plan with the teachers so that you demonstrate to pupils your commitment to team work?	8	4
4. Do you have plans that encourage constructive feedback to each other?	8	3
5. Are there agreed plans for your response to individual pupils? (e.g. If X happens we must say... If Y happens we must do...etc)	8	4
6. Do you contribute to class records? The following ways of contributing were given: Feedback sheets, target folders, guided reading, annual reviews, liaising with class teacher, observations.	10	2
7. Are you asked to comment informally on pupils' progress?	12	0
8. Are you asked about classroom arrangements?	8	4
9. Do you contribute to the evidence of formal assessment? (e.g. reports, statements, annual reviews, etc.)	11	1
10. Do you have an appropriate job description? 4 people also said yes when re-written and 1 was unsure.	5	2

11. Do you think being involved in writing your own job
description has been a positive experience? 11 1
Some of the ways LSAs said: It helps to clarify roles
and have opinions valued.
Opportunity to discuss as a team and reflect on role.
Analyse my role thoroughly, and focus on all areas
of my job.
Helps to update increased work load.

12. How often has your job description been reviewed?
7 said never
2 said once
1st time in 5 years
not often

13. How often do you think a job description should
be reviewed?
7 said yearly.
4 said every 2/3 years.
1 said every 5 years.

14. Do you have any comments that would help fulfil
your role? 9 3
Suggestions were:
Allocated time with class teacher for planning &
evaluation.
Time to make resources and record child/ren's progress.
Being involved in planning every week.
Handover period for job share.
Further training – behaviour management.
1 LSA per year group.

15. How much NCT do you have including Assemblies:
NCT almost all LSAs had none.
Assemblies 3 LSAs have shared time, whilst 2 said
they are free once maybe twice a week.

16. Do you feel that the whole school community
understands your job?
e.g. Teachers 10 2
    Parents 5 6
    Pupils 10 1

17. Does your contract specify preparation time?
3 no answers.

18. Do you think Professional Development Interviews
    are useful?   11   1
    LSAs said yes because:
    Helps to assess my performance in the classroom.
    Any problems can be discussed.
    To express concerns.
    Opportunity to focus & evaluate job & contributions.
    Allows LSAs to consider future development
    Enables senior staff to review policies on LSAs.
    Discuss progression & improve on weaknesses.
    Identify training needs.

19. Planning time is often an issue. If you had time to
    plan together in school day when would be appropriate?
    Suggestions were:
            Lunchtime (7)
            Assembly time (2)

Training

1. Were you provided with a school induction programme? 1   10

2. An induction programme would be beneficial,
   but would you write down the 3 most important
   things you would like the programme to include.

   Most important things included:

   a. Mentor – someone to show a new person around
      the school and where things can be found, etc.,
      and who's who.
   b. Training opportunities.
   c. Meeting with SENCO – explanation of system
      of statementing and IEPs and all specialists
      involved with child/ren.
   d. Explanation of safety and emergency procedures.
   e. Introduction to whole staff.

WHITMORE HIGH

A SURVEY OF LEARNING ASSISTANTS' VIEWS

	Not at all	Not much	Just OK	Pretty much	Very much
* Clear about roles and responsibilities	0	1	2	8	1
* Valued as part of the Learning Support Department	0	1	2	8	1
* Given regular opportunities for planning with teacher colleagues	6	5	1	0	0
* Clear about learning objectives	1	3	2	6	0
* Deployed efficiently, effectively, flexibly	0	2	2	8	0
* Given opportunities for training and development	0	2	2	8	0

Appendix 7
Job descriptions

RYLES PARK HIGH

Job Description

Name:	Carolyn Ashcroft
Job Title:	Teaching Assistant
Grade:	
Hours P/W:	32.5 hours per week
School:	Ryles Park High School, Macclesfield
Accountable to:	

Job Purpose: To enhance the learning of pupils who have a wide range of learning needs; by supporting the teaching staff in enabling the pupils to gain independence and participate fully in the curriculum and general life of the school. To be adaptable, have empathy but also follow the school's 'positive discipline' guidelines.

Duties and Responsibilities

Support for the pupil

Central to the whole principle of inclusion – those children who have learning or physical difficulties should be helped to work independently in the company of other children across the curriculum.

Support for the teachers

To develop a mutually supportive relationship with all teaching staff. Endeavour to help pupils gain access to the curriculum by differentiating instructions and resources. Assisting pupils to become better learners by discreetly prompting them to stay 'on task'.

Support for the curriculum

Support the delivery of the Literacy and Mathematics strategy along with other aspects of both the National Curriculum and the enhanced curriculum offered by school.

Support for the school

To work as part of a flexible and supportive team to further the ethos of the school. To undertake relevant training to enhance personal development and to use the knowledge to benefit the school. To attend 1/2 termly TA meetings to develop and disseminate good practice.

Key accountabilities:

- The management and administration of SuccessMaker. Duties include: enrolling pupils, monitoring their individual progress, designing and producing certificates which acknowledge their effort and progress, ensuring the smooth running of the programme, generating reports and homework throughout the school year, contact with parents.
- To continue as the link liaison person within the mathematics department by attending all relevant meetings, held both in and out of school. This role also includes involvement in the mathematics pilot scheme.

Signature of post holder ....

Signature of line manager ....

Date ....

I wish the following contributions to the school community to be recognised:

- Lunch time – ICT/Homework club – 1 session plus support/cover at additional sessions.
- Designing and producing colour co-ordinated, laminated magnetic 'Key Words' for mathematics department.
- The set-up and organisation of SuccessMaker for the literacy/mathematics Summer Schools at Ryles Park.
- Attend Year 7 'Parents Evenings' in order to inform parents about their children's progress on SuccessMaker.
- Attend 'Open Evenings' to explain the role of SuccessMaker within Ryles Park School.
- Involvement with Manchester University/DfEE 'Research Project' regarding the role of Teaching Assistants.
- Facilitate evening opportunities for parents to experience SuccessMaker with their children.
- Support the 'Learning Through Computers, Introductory Evening Courses' for interested parents during the Summer term.
- Evening – supporting ICT/Homework club 1 session each week.

Key Accountabilities and Personal Contributions sections of the job description will be reviewed annually by .... (appointed member of staff) to allow for any amendments that you may wish to make.

I may be required to do any of the following tasks on a daily basis:

- Supporting individual students and whole classes across the full curriculum.
- Support a Registration Class and carry out associated duties.

- Mentoring: supporting individual students with emotional and behavioural problems.
- Exam invigilation, amanuensis and assistance.
- Prepare and teach literacy/mathematics lessons to small groups of pupils.
- Displaying students' work to create a stimulating environment and raise students' self-esteem.
- Rewarding and disciplining students in accordance with the School's policy of 'Positive Discipline', e.g. writing and sending 'good news cards', issuing merit marks, phone calls home, good and mis-conduct forms.
- Following up 'late' or 'missing' students.
- Withdrawing and escorting disruptive students to SMT as and when necessary (usually at teacher's request).
- Recording class notes for students who attend Speech/Physiotherapy sessions.
- Photocopying and differentiating resources and worksheets.
- Assisting with the setting up and clearing away of equipment in practical areas.
- Accompanying student on Educational trips 'off site'.
- Attending and participating in meetings: whole school and departmental.
- Undertaking training in order to upgrade/learn skills as required.
- Participate in INSET days.

PARKES FIELD SCHOOL

Parkes Field School

Job Description:
Title: Teaching Assistant (Grant 32)
Role: To support the pupils at Parkes Field School by meeting their care needs and by assisting the teaching staff in meeting their learning needs.

Main Duties:
Supporting the pupils
- To supervise and support pupils in a variety of learning and social contexts
- To work with pupils in the classroom, individually or in small groups
- To support pupils during inclusion placements at local mainstream school
- To establish a supportive and trusting relationship with the pupils
- To develop appropriate resources to support the pupils
- To supervise pupils in the bathroom and assist in the development of independence and self-care skills
- To supervise pupils during break times
- To facilitate appropriate movement of children within the moving and handling guidelines

Supporting the curriculum
- To develop a knowledge of Literacy, Numeracy and other National Curriculum subjects relevant to the pupils' abilities
- To develop a broad knowledge of special needs and how teaching methods are adapted to meet these needs
- To develop and adapt resources to support the curriculum
- To facilitate pupils' access to the curriculum

Supporting the teacher
- To assist the class teacher and other professionals in the delivery of the curriculum
- To contribute to the maintenance of pupils' workbooks and records
- To provide relevant feedback about pupils to the teacher
- To take part in class or pupil planning meetings when required
- To prepare classroom equipment, work and resources and tidy as appropriate

Supporting the school
- To attend relevant in-service training
- To liaise and consult with other members of the team
- To be aware of school procedures
- To maintain confidentiality
- To maintain links between home and school via take-home books
- To undertake duties, falling within the remit of this post, at the discretion of the Head teacher

Responsible to Mrs Edwards Head teacher
             Mrs Monks Assistant Head teacher and mentor

Appendix 8 Planning analysis

HARROW VI SERVICE

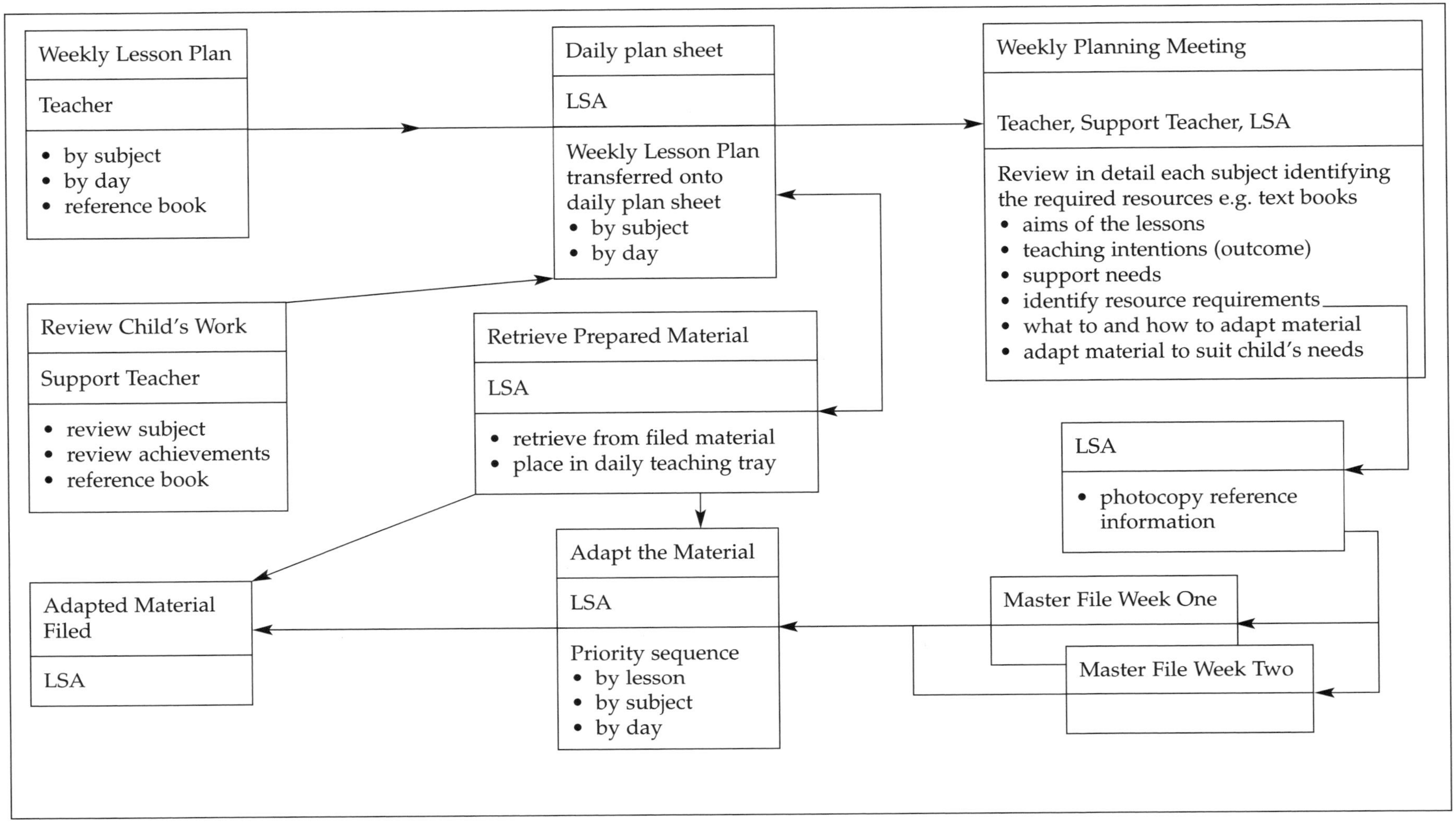

Weekly Planning Meeting

Teacher, Support Teacher, LSA

Review in detail each subject identifying the required resources e.g. text books
- aims of the lessons
- teaching intentions (outcome)
- support needs
- identify resource requirements
- what to and how to adapt material
- adapt material to suit child's needs

Daily plan sheet

LSA

Weekly Lesson Plan transferred onto daily plan sheet
- by subject
- by day

Weekly Lesson Plan

Teacher
- by subject
- by day
- reference book

Retrieve Prepared Material

LSA
- retrieve from filed material
- place in daily teaching tray

Review Child's Work

Support Teacher
- review subject
- review achievements
- reference book

Adapt the Material

LSA

Priority sequence
- by lesson
- by subject
- by day

Adapted Material Filed

LSA

LSA
- photocopy reference information

Master File Week One

Master File Week Two

Appendix 9 Detailed curriculum planning

HARROW VI TEAM

High School Geography Department KS3 Unit: Tectonic Activity (earth's structure, volcanoes, earthquakes)

Key Knowledge	Scale	Duration (Approx)	Key Concepts	Skills	Teaching Strategy/ Assessment	Resources	Homework
Types of damage and devastation caused by volcanoes and earthquakes	local	10 mins	Natural hazards cause different types of damage and devastation	• interpreting photos*	• **In pairs**† study photos on pp. 66 & 67 • *Geography Direct* ✿ • List effects shown in photos. • **Class feedback/ Spider diagram**†	• *Geography Direct*	
• Use of seismographs • Knowledge of Richter and Mercalli Scales	global	30 mins	• Methods of measuring earthquakes • Prediction is not 100% accurate	• Numeracy skills • interpreting graphs*	Study information on p.76 ✿ *Geography Direct* Do Q.1a, b & c. Q.2 & 3 Optional	• *Geography Direct*	Draw and annotate a diagram to show damage expected at different magnitudes on the Richter Scale
• Cause of damage devastation from earthquakes	global	1 lesson	Secondary effects usually cause more death and damage than actual tremors	• processing information	• **Watch earthquake video**† • Make a list of the different causes of death and damage	*Earthquakes video*	Choose 5 causes of damage from the list made. How could each one be prevented?
Earthquakes are caused by friction from plates rubbing/ crashing together	local	1 lesson	• Kobe case study • Causes of earthquakes revision	• Interpreting maps* • numeracy skills	Read p.80 *Geography Direct* Do Q.3a, b, c. ✿	*Geography Direct*	

† See teacher

✿ Enlarge/Braille

* Make/given written explanations

References

Balshaw, M. H. (1991) *Help in the Classroom*. London: David Fulton Publishers.

Balshaw, M. H. (1999) *Help in the Classroom*, 2nd edn. London: David Fulton Publishers.

Booth, T. and Ainscow, M. (eds) (1998) *From Them to Us: An International Study of Inclusion in Education*. London: Routledge.

Clery, E. (2001) 'Planning: its importance in the work of learning support assistants', *Visability* (Spring 2001). RNIB.

CSIE (2000) *Learning Supporters and Inclusion*. Bristol: Centre for Studies on Inclusive Education.

DES (1978) *Special Educational Needs* (The Warnock Report). London: DES Publications.

DfEE (1997) *Excellence for All Children: Meeting Special Educational Needs*. London: DfEE Publications.

DfEE (1998) *Teachers: Meeting the Challenge of Change*. London: DfEE Publications.

DfEE (2000a) *Working with Teaching Assistants: A Good Practice Guide*. London: DfEE Publications.

DfEE (2000b) *Induction Training for Teaching Assistants (Primary)*. London: DfEE Publications.

DfES (2001) *Induction Training for Teaching Assistants (Secondary)*. London: DfES Publications.

Farrell, P., Balshaw, M. and Polat, F. (1999) *The Management, Role and Training of Learning Support Assistants*. London: DfEE Publications.

Fox, G. (1993) *A Handbook for Special Needs Assistants*. London: David Fulton Publishers.

Fox, G. (1998) *A Handbook for Learning Support Assistants*. London: David Fulton Publishers.

Jupp, K. (1992) *Everyone Belongs*. London: Souvenir Press.

Lee, B. and Mawson, C. (1998) *Survey of Classroom Assistants*. Slough: NFER.

LGNTO (2001) *National Occupational Standards for Teaching Assistants*. Local Government National Training Organisation.

Lorenz, S. (1998) *Effective In-Class Support*. London: David Fulton Publishers.

Mencap (1999) *On a Wing and a Prayer: Inclusion and Children with Severe Learning Difficulties*. Mencap.

Ofsted (2000) *Inspecting Schools: The Framework*. London: Office for Standards in Education.

Rose, R. (2000) 'Using classroom support in the primary school', *British Journal of Special Education* 27, 4: 191–6.

Smith, K., Kenner, C. and Barton-Hide, M. (1999) *Career Ladders for Classroom Assistants*, University of Southampton and Hampshire County Council.

TTA (2001) *Progression to Initial Teacher Training for Teaching Assistants*. Teacher Training Agency.

Thomas, G., Walker, D. and Webb, J. (1998) *The Making of an Inclusive School*. London: Routledge.

Unesco (1991) *Special Needs in the Classroom: A Teacher Education Resource Pack*. Paris: Unesco.